SPECTRUM®

Division

Grade 4

Spectrum®
An imprint of Carson-Dellosa Publishing LLC
P.O. Box 35665
Greensboro, NC 27425 USA

ISBN 978-1-4838-0477-4

06-100171151

Table of Contents Grade 4

Spectrum Division is designed to build a solid foundation in division for your fourth grader. Aligned to the fourth grade Common Core State Standards for division, every page equips your child with the confidence to master division. Helpful examples provide step-by-step guidance to teach new concepts, followed by a variety of practice pages that will sharpen your child's skills and efficiency at problem solving. Use the Pretests, Posttests, Mid-Test, and Final Test as the perfect way to track your child's progress and identify where he or she needs extra practice.

Common Core State Standards Alignment: Division Grade 4

Domain: Operations and Algebraic Thinking	
Standard	Aligned Practice Pages
3.OA.2	29, 30–31, 33, 36, 38, 81
3.OA.3	25–36, 38, 67–76, 80–82
4.OA.5	13, 17, 21, 23, 34, 79
Domain: Number and Operations in Base Ten	
Standard	Aligned Practice Pages
4.NBT.1	39, 62–63, 66, 71, 77–78, 80
4.NBT.3	65, 75, 82
4.NBT.6	5–82

NAME _____

 # Check What You Know

Division Facts through 81 ÷ 9

Divide.

	a	b	c	d	e
1.	3)15	7)49	9)27	5)45	7)21
2.	3)18	7)42	9)81	7)56	6)30
3.	4)36	4)16	5)40	2)10	4)36
4.	9)18	5)35	7)28	2)6	4)24
5.	5)15	3)21	9)54	2)8	2)14
6.	6)36	6)48	8)32	3)24	3)9
7.	8)72	8)64	5)25	9)9	3)0
8.	5)35	5)20	4)36	8)56	2)12
9.	2)18	3)27	4)28	2)2	2)8
10.	3)15	9)63	6)48	7)14	9)27

Spectrum Division
Grade 4

Chapter 1
Division Facts through 81 ÷ 9

Dividing through 45 ÷ 5

$$9 \longleftarrow \text{quotient}$$

divisor $\longrightarrow 5\overline{)45} \longleftarrow$ dividend

To check your answer, do the inverse operation.

If $45 \div 5 = 9$, then $5 \times 9 = 45$ must be true.

Using the division table, find 45 in the 5 column. The quotient is named at the beginning of the row.

5-column ⟶ ↓ **(divisors)**

(quotients)

×	0	1	2	3	4	5	6	7	8	9
0	0	0	0	0	0	0	0	0	0	0
1	0	1	2	3	4	5	6	7	8	9
2	0	2	4	6	8	10	12	14	16	18
3	0	3	6	9	12	15	18	21	24	27
4	0	4	8	12	16	20	24	28	32	36
5	0	5	10	15	20	25	30	35	40	45
6	0	6	12	18	24	30	36	42	48	54
7	0	7	14	21	28	35	42	49	56	63
8	0	8	16	24	32	40	48	56	64	72
9	0	9	18	27	36	45	54	63	72	81

quotient ⟶

Divide.

	a	b	c	d	e
1.	$5\overline{)35}$	$4\overline{)16}$	$4\overline{)36}$	$3\overline{)18}$	$5\overline{)25}$
2.	$2\overline{)18}$	$3\overline{)18}$	$3\overline{)27}$	$3\overline{)12}$	$5\overline{)20}$
3.	$5\overline{)45}$	$3\overline{)15}$	$5\overline{)30}$	$4\overline{)32}$	$2\overline{)8}$

Complete the following.

	a	b	c
	a	b	c

4.

a.
$$\begin{array}{r} 5 \\ \times 3 \\ \hline 15 \end{array}$$ so $3\overline{)15}$

b.
$$\begin{array}{r} 4 \\ \times 7 \\ \hline 28 \end{array}$$ so $7\overline{)28}$

c.
$$\begin{array}{r} 3 \\ \times 4 \\ \hline 12 \end{array}$$ so $4\overline{)12}$

NAME _____

SCORE ⬭ **/23**

Dividing through 45 ÷ 5

Divide.

	a	b	c	d	e
1.	3)$\overline{21}$	2)$\overline{10}$	2)$\overline{16}$	2)$\overline{12}$	9)$\overline{45}$
2.	5)$\overline{35}$	2)$\overline{18}$	5)$\overline{40}$	5)$\overline{30}$	4)$\overline{24}$
3.	3)$\overline{24}$	4)$\overline{20}$	3)$\overline{9}$	4)$\overline{12}$	2)$\overline{14}$
4.	4)$\overline{4}$	5)$\overline{15}$	5)$\overline{10}$	4)$\overline{0}$	3)$\overline{6}$

Complete the following.

	a	b	c
5.	4 ×6 ――― 24 so 6)$\overline{24}$	3 ×8 ――― 24 so 8)$\overline{24}$	5 ×6 ――― 30 so 6)$\overline{30}$

Dividing through 63 ÷ 7

$$9 \longleftarrow \text{quotient}$$

divisor $\longrightarrow 7\overline{)63} \longleftarrow$ dividend

To check your answer, do the inverse operation.

If $63 \div 7 = 9$, then $7 \times 9 = 63$ must be true.

Using the division table, find 63 in the 7 column. The quotient is named at the end of the row.

7-column $\longrightarrow$

x	0	1	2	3	4	5	6	7	8	9
0	0	0	0	0	0	0	0	0	0	0
1	0	1	2	3	4	5	6	7	8	9
2	0	2	4	6	8	10	12	14	16	18
3	0	3	6	9	12	15	18	21	24	27
4	0	4	8	12	16	20	24	28	32	36
5	0	5	10	15	20	25	30	35	40	45
6	0	6	12	18	24	30	36	42	48	54
7	0	7	14	21	28	35	42	49	56	63
8	0	8	16	24	32	40	48	56	64	72
9	0	9	18	27	36	45	54	63	72	81

quotient

Divide.

	a	b	c	d	e
1.	$7\overline{)49}$	$5\overline{)45}$	$6\overline{)36}$	$3\overline{)24}$	$3\overline{)27}$
2.	$2\overline{)18}$	$4\overline{)24}$	$6\overline{)48}$	$4\overline{)32}$	$5\overline{)45}$
3.	$5\overline{)40}$	$2\overline{)12}$	$6\overline{)6}$	$7\overline{)56}$	$7\overline{)0}$

Complete the following.

	a	b	c
4.	$\begin{array}{r} 7 \\ \times 6 \\ \hline 42 \end{array}$ so $6\overline{)42}$	$\begin{array}{r} 5 \\ \times 9 \\ \hline 45 \end{array}$ so $9\overline{)45}$	$\begin{array}{r} 8 \\ \times 7 \\ \hline 56 \end{array}$ so $7\overline{)56}$

Dividing through 63 ÷ 7

Divide.

	a	b	c	d	e
1.	2)16	6)54	5)25	5)10	7)21
2.	7)28	6)42	7)63	6)24	4)20
3.	7)35	5)30	4)12	4)16	7)7
4.	5)15	7)42	3)21	6)12	6)30

Complete the following.

	a	b	c

5.

a.
  6
× 9
___
5 4 so 9)5 4

b.
  7
× 4
___
2 8 so 4)2 8

c.
  7
× 9
___
6 3 so 9)6 3

Dividing through 81 ÷ 9

$$9 \leftarrow \text{quotient}$$

divisor ⟶ $9\overline{)81}$ ⟵ dividend

To check your answer, do the inverse operation.

If $81 \div 9 = 9$, then $9 \times 9 = 81$ must be true.

Using the division table, find 81 in the 9 column. The quotient is named at the end of the row.

9-column

x	0	1	2	3	4	5	6	7	8	9
0	0	0	0	0	0	0	0	0	0	0
1	0	1	2	3	4	5	6	7	8	9
2	0	2	4	6	8	10	12	14	16	18
3	0	3	6	9	12	15	18	21	24	27
4	0	4	8	12	16	20	24	28	32	36
5	0	5	10	15	20	25	30	35	40	45
6	0	6	12	18	24	30	36	42	48	54
7	0	7	14	21	28	35	42	49	56	63
8	0	8	16	24	32	40	48	56	64	72
9	0	9	18	27	36	45	54	63	72	81

quotient

Divide.

	a	b	c	d	e
1.	$9\overline{)72}$	$8\overline{)40}$	$8\overline{)24}$	$6\overline{)48}$	$7\overline{)28}$
2.	$6\overline{)18}$	$3\overline{)21}$	$7\overline{)49}$	$9\overline{)54}$	$9\overline{)81}$
3.	$5\overline{)35}$	$7\overline{)56}$	$9\overline{)18}$	$7\overline{)42}$	$9\overline{)36}$

Complete the following.

	a	b	c
4.	$\begin{array}{r} 7 \\ \times 5 \\ \hline 35 \end{array}$ so $5\overline{)35}$	$\begin{array}{r} 8 \\ \times 8 \\ \hline 64 \end{array}$ so $8\overline{)64}$	$\begin{array}{r} 9 \\ \times 6 \\ \hline 54 \end{array}$ so $6\overline{)54}$

Dividing through 81 ÷ 9

Divide.

	a	b	c	d	e
1.	$7\overline{)42}$	$5\overline{)45}$	$8\overline{)32}$	$7\overline{)63}$	$8\overline{)64}$
2.	$6\overline{)36}$	$4\overline{)32}$	$7\overline{)28}$	$9\overline{)0}$	$4\overline{)28}$
3.	$9\overline{)45}$	$5\overline{)30}$	$4\overline{)12}$	$5\overline{)25}$	$7\overline{)14}$
4.	$9\overline{)9}$	$8\overline{)40}$	$8\overline{)48}$	$6\overline{)42}$	$3\overline{)27}$

Complete the following.

	a	b	c
5.	$\begin{array}{r} 9 \\ \times 4 \\ \hline 36 \end{array}$ so $4\overline{)36}$	$\begin{array}{r} 7 \\ \times 9 \\ \hline 63 \end{array}$ so $9\overline{)63}$	$\begin{array}{r} 6 \\ \times 8 \\ \hline 48 \end{array}$ so $8\overline{)48}$

Division Practice

Divide.

	a	b	c	d	e
1.	8)56	6)24	2)18	5)35	7)42
2.	6)48	6)30	8)72	6)36	9)81
3.	9)54	3)21	7)28	3)18	2)18
4.	5)45	9)36	6)42	8)64	7)63
5.	3)24	9)27	5)20	7)49	5)25

Division Practice

Divide.

	a	b	c	d	e
1.	3)9	2)4	3)6	4)8	1)7
2.	3)0	2)10	7)14	2)6	3)54
3.	1)5	3)12	6)12	2)2	5)10
4.	5)25	4)16	3)15	8)72	2)2

Find the rule and complete each table.

a

In	Out
21	
35	5
63	
49	
14	2

b

In	Out
12	
10	5
14	
18	9
22	

c

In	Out
81	
36	4
54	
72	8
9	

5.

_____   _____   _____

Division Practice

Divide.

	a	b	c	d	e
1.	$4\overline{)28}$	$4\overline{)4}$	$2\overline{)18}$	$6\overline{)18}$	$9\overline{)63}$
2.	$7\overline{)63}$	$3\overline{)27}$	$4\overline{)32}$	$8\overline{)64}$	$8\overline{)48}$
3.	$4\overline{)24}$	$9\overline{)72}$	$8\overline{)32}$	$5\overline{)20}$	$9\overline{)45}$
4.	$6\overline{)24}$	$7\overline{)49}$	$9\overline{)81}$	$5\overline{)30}$	$3\overline{)21}$
5.	$8\overline{)16}$	$2\overline{)8}$	$7\overline{)28}$	$7\overline{)42}$	$6\overline{)48}$

Division Practice

Divide.

	a	b	c	d	e
1.	$5\overline{)30}$	$7\overline{)21}$	$4\overline{)28}$	$9\overline{)63}$	$5\overline{)35}$
2.	$1\overline{)9}$	$4\overline{)24}$	$8\overline{)32}$	$6\overline{)36}$	$2\overline{)14}$
3.	$7\overline{)56}$	$4\overline{)36}$	$9\overline{)27}$	$6\overline{)42}$	$8\overline{)8}$
4.	$3\overline{)24}$	$7\overline{)63}$	$9\overline{)54}$	$3\overline{)27}$	$1\overline{)7}$
5.	$8\overline{)24}$	$2\overline{)16}$	$7\overline{)42}$	$6\overline{)54}$	$8\overline{)56}$

Division Practice

Divide.

	a	b	c	d	e
1.	$3\overline{)15}$	$8\overline{)40}$	$3\overline{)21}$	$9\overline{)36}$	$4\overline{)20}$
2.	$8\overline{)32}$	$9\overline{)9}$	$5\overline{)35}$	$9\overline{)81}$	$6\overline{)36}$
3.	$4\overline{)32}$	$8\overline{)64}$	$1\overline{)4}$	$7\overline{)42}$	$7\overline{)28}$
4.	$6\overline{)30}$	$3\overline{)24}$	$6\overline{)48}$	$9\overline{)54}$	$3\overline{)18}$
5.	$8\overline{)72}$	$6\overline{)24}$	$8\overline{)56}$	$7\overline{)35}$	$4\overline{)28}$

Division Practice

Divide.

	a	b	c	d	e
1.	6)48	7)28	7)42	8)56	6)24
2.	5)35	8)64	6)30	9)63	7)49
3.	8)40	9)54	4)32	5)45	7)56
4.	4)36	5)30	7)63	8)72	7)35

Find the rule and complete each table.

a

In	Out
12	4
30	
21	
18	
9	3

b

In	Out
32	
48	
16	2
56	7
24	

c

In	Out
24	6
36	
12	3
28	
20	

5.

_____   _____   _____

Division Practice

Divide.

	a	b	c	d	e
1.	6)48	4)32	6)36	7)42	7)28
2.	9)45	8)56	6)30	9)54	7)49
3.	5)35	6)24	9)36	8)40	9)63
4.	7)21	6)54	4)20	8)32	7)56
5.	3)21	5)40	5)20	5)45	7)35

Division Practice

Divide.

	a	b	c	d	e
1.	4)̄12	3)̄15	2)̄18	6)̄24	3)̄21
2.	5)̄25	4)̄16	5)̄20	7)̄14	8)̄8
3.	4)̄32	6)̄30	3)̄27	8)̄16	8)̄24
4.	9)̄18	4)̄24	5)̄5	7)̄28	1)̄5
5.	4)̄36	1)̄9	7)̄21	5)̄15	9)̄36

Division Practice

Divide.

	a	b	c	d	e
1.	4)36	6)54	4)8	8)16	2)12
2.	6)18	9)81	4)4	6)30	3)9
3.	7)14	3)21	5)40	3)24	4)16
4.	1)5	3)6	5)10	4)12	5)30
5.	7)49	9)63	4)32	2)14	1)8

Division Practice

Divide.

	a	b	c	d	e
1.	$5\overline{)20}$	$1\overline{)8}$	$7\overline{)7}$	$3\overline{)27}$	$5\overline{)35}$
2.	$8\overline{)40}$	$7\overline{)21}$	$9\overline{)45}$	$7\overline{)42}$	$8\overline{)64}$
3.	$2\overline{)18}$	$3\overline{)15}$	$6\overline{)12}$	$6\overline{)24}$	$8\overline{)48}$
4.	$6\overline{)6}$	$2\overline{)8}$	$9\overline{)36}$	$4\overline{)20}$	$2\overline{)16}$

Find the rule and complete each table.

5.

a

In	Out
30	
40	8
25	
45	9
20	

b

In	Out
8	
64	8
24	
56	7
40	

c

In	Out
36	
18	
54	
42	7
12	2

_____   _____   _____

Division Practice

Divide.

	a	b	c	d	e
1.	$1\overline{)4}$	$2\overline{)16}$	$9\overline{)63}$	$7\overline{)42}$	$5\overline{)20}$
2.	$9\overline{)54}$	$9\overline{)9}$	$4\overline{)12}$	$1\overline{)6}$	$9\overline{)36}$
3.	$8\overline{)16}$	$5\overline{)25}$	$2\overline{)12}$	$4\overline{)8}$	$3\overline{)6}$
4.	$8\overline{)8}$	$6\overline{)30}$	$6\overline{)18}$	$6\overline{)54}$	$9\overline{)27}$
5.	$2\overline{)14}$	$2\overline{)10}$	$1\overline{)3}$	$4\overline{)20}$	$3\overline{)18}$

NAME _____

SCORE ⬭ / 25

Division Practice

Divide.

	a	b	c	d	e
1.	8)72	2)6	7)56	3)24	4)32
2.	7)63	4)16	8)32	5)30	2)8
3.	7)7	8)24	3)27	6)6	1)8
4.	5)35	6)42	6)36	8)64	3)21

Find the rule and complete each table.

5.

a

In	Out
18	
45	
63	7
36	
27	3

b

In	Out
21	7
6	
24	
27	9
15	

c

In	Out
7	
42	
35	5
56	8
49	

_____   _____   _____

NAME _____

 Check What You Learned

Division Facts through 81 ÷ 9

Divide.

	a	b	c	d	e
1.	3)18	9)27	7)7	8)64	5)40
2.	9)72	6)36	8)16	7)21	4)28
3.	5)25	8)64	9)54	5)35	3)12
4.	7)49	9)9	7)21	2)18	3)18
5.	4)16	4)20	9)36	8)56	7)42
6.	9)0	4)32	9)81	5)10	7)49
7.	8)32	9)54	6)48	3)24	4)24
8.	9)45	3)27	5)30	6)42	2)4
9.	8)40	9)63	2)14	3)9	7)56
10.	8)48	7)7	2)8	1)9	7)28

CHAPTER 1 POSTTEST

Check What You Know

Problem Solving: Division Facts through 81 ÷ 9

Read the problem carefully and solve. Show your work under each question.

Darnell collects stickers. He wants to organize them in a sticker book. He plans to put the same number of stickers on each page. Darnell has 24 sports stickers, 81 animal stickers, 36 fuzzy stickers, and 63 scratch-and-sniff stickers.

1. Darnell can fit 9 animal stickers on a page. How many pages will he use for his animal stickers?

_____ pages

2. Darnell puts all of his scratch-and-sniff stickers on 7 pages. He puts the same number of stickers on each page. How many stickers are on each page?

_____ stickers

3. Darnell fits all of his sports stickers onto 3 pages. If each page has the same number of stickers, how many stickers are on each page? What multiplication sentence can Darnell use to check his division?

_____ stickers

_____

4. How many pages will Darnell use for his fuzzy stickers if he puts 6 fuzzy stickers on each page?

_____ pages

SCORE ⬤ /3

Dividing through 45 ÷ 5

Read the problem carefully and solve. Show your work under each question.

Carolyn helps get 4 sailboats ready for a sailing class. She divides the supplies evenly between each sailboat. She has 8 sails and 20 life jackets. All of the sailboats need new ropes for their sails. There are 16 pieces of rope.

Helpful Hint

The division sentence 16 ÷ 2 = 8 can also be written as:

quotient ⟶ 8
divisor ⟶ 2 $\overline{)1\,6}$ ⟵ dividend

1. Carolyn puts the same number of sails on each boat. How many sails does she put on each sailboat?

   _____ sails

2. The pieces of rope are evenly divided among the boats. How many pieces of rope does each sailboat get?

   _____ pieces of rope

3. Carolyn puts the same number of life jackets on each boat. How many life jackets does she put on each boat?

   _____ life jackets

SCORE ⬭ **/3**

Dividing through 63 ÷ 7

Read the problem carefully and solve. Show your work under each question.

Michael coaches a tennis program at a summer camp. He divides the campers into 2 teams, beginners and advanced. He has 54 tennis balls to use with the beginner team and 48 balls to use with the advanced team. He always divides the tennis balls evenly between the groups within each team.

1. Michael divides the beginners into 6 groups for a practice drill. How many tennis balls does each group get?

_____ tennis balls

2. Michael divides the advanced players into 6 groups to practice serving. How many tennis balls does each group get?

_____ tennis balls

3. The beginners lost 5 tennis balls. Michael divides the players into 7 groups for the next activity. How many tennis balls will each group get?

_____ tennis balls

SCORE ⬤ / 4

Dividing through 81 ÷ 9

Read the problem carefully and solve. Show your work under each question.

Carla fills baskets with flowers for her mom's surprise birthday party. Each of the 8 tables will get a basket. There are 72 pink flowers, 56 yellow flowers, and 64 white flowers. Carla wants to divide the flowers evenly between the baskets.

Helpful Hint

When solving word problems, write an equation to help you find the answer. If you know there are 63 total items to be equally divided between 9 people and you want to know how many items each person gets, you can write the problem like this:

$63 \div x = 9$

Then, find x by finding the number that makes 63 when multiplied by 9.

$9 \times 7 = 63$ $x = 7$

---

1. Carla evenly divides the pink flowers among the baskets. How many pink flowers are in each basket?

_____ pink flowers

2. Carla notices 16 of the white flowers are too wilted to use. If Carla throws those flowers away, how many white flowers are in each basket? Write a division equation. Then, solve.

_____   _____ white flowers

3. After Carla evenly divides the yellow flowers between the baskets, she wants to check to make sure she divided correctly. What multiplication sentence can Carla use to check her work?

_____

Division Practice

Read the problem carefully and solve. Show your work under each question.

Appleton School is having a cake and cookie sale. Students are helping to bake the cakes and cookies. They measure and mix the recipes.

1. Delores divides flour into batches to make cakes. She has 18 cups of flour. Each cake takes 2 cups. How many cakes can she make?

_____ cakes

2. Ella has 21 teaspoons of vanilla. Each batch of cookies takes 3 teaspoons. How many batches of cookies can Ella make from this much vanilla?

_____ batches

3. Each batch of cookies contains 8 tablespoons of chopped pecans. Marty has 40 tablespoons of chopped pecans. How many batches of cookies can she make with the pecans?

_____ batches

Division Practice

Solve each problem. Show your work under each question.

1. Mrs. Blair is planning a yard party. Her big punch bowl holds 40 glasses of punch. If she wants to allow 5 glasses for each guest, how many guests will the punch bowl serve?

The punch bowl will serve _____ guests.

2. At the rodeo, 32 people signed up for bronco riding. The 4 horses will give the same number of rides. How many rides will each horse give? Write a division equation. Then, solve.

_____

Each horse will give _____ rides.

3. Mr. Ferris is packing to move to a new house. He has 35 pairs of shoes. He can pack 7 pairs of shoes in a box. How many boxes will he need for his shoes?

Mr. Ferris will need _____ boxes for his shoes.

Division Practice

Solve each problem. Show your work under each question.

1. At the local fair, 72 people waited in line for a boat ride. The boat can hold 8 people. How many trips will the boat have to take for everyone to get a ride?

   The boat will have to take _____ trips.

2. The Davis brothers found 27 cars when they cleaned out their toy closet. They want to give the same number of cars to each of their 3 cousins. How many cars will each cousin get?

   Each cousin will get _____ toy cars.

3. Mrs. Gomez sold 18 pet lizards this week at her pet store. If 9 customers bought the same number of lizards, how many lizards did each person take home? Write a division equation. Then, solve.

   _____

   Each person took home _____ lizards.

Division Practice

Solve each problem. Show your work under each question.

1. Eddie and Toru listened to 72 of their favorite songs. If there were 9 songs on each CD, how many CDs did they listen to?

They listened to _____ CDs.

2. Mr. Luiz printed 35 tests for his students. If there were 7 rows of students, how many tests were passed out to each row?

There were _____ tests passed out to each row.

3. Gary opened a bag of candy containing 81 pieces. He wants to give each of his guests the same number of pieces. If he has 9 guests, how many pieces does each person get?

Each guest gets _____ pieces.

SCORE ⬭ / 3

Division Practice

Solve each problem. Show your work under each question.

1. Last year, Mrs. Ford decided to give chores to each person in the family. Each person got the same number of chores. There are 8 family members. If there were 32 chores, how many did each person get?

Each person got _____ chores.

2. It takes 16 hours to drive to the dunes. Tasha and her brother Kurt will drive the same number of hours. How many hours will each of them drive?

Each of them will drive _____ hours.

3. The Pet Store warehouse received 63 boxes of cat litter. The same number of boxes will be sent to 9 stores. How many boxes will each store get? Write a division equation. Then, solve.

_____

Each store will get _____ boxes.

Division Practice

Solve each problem. Show your work under each question.

1. Lori found 42 shells at the beach. She gave the same number of shells to 7 of her friends. How many shells did she give to each friend?

   She gave _____ shells to each friend.

2. The drama club is giving a party in the school lunchroom. The club wants to be seated in groups of 8. If 64 students go to the party, how many groups of students will there be?

   The drama club will have _____ groups of students.

3. The Pancake Restaurant served 32 pancakes. If 8 customers ate an equal number of pancakes, how many did each person eat?

   Each person ate _____ pancakes.

Division Practice

Solve each problem. Show your work under each question.

1. In the flower seed package, there are 48 seeds. Alicia has 8 flowerpots. She wants to put an equal number of seeds in each pot. How many seeds should she put in each pot?

She should put _____ seeds in each pot.

2. The local baseball team has a supply of 54 baseballs for 9 home games. How many baseballs are available for each home game?

There are _____ baseballs available for each home game.

3. The class gerbil has just had 16 babies. If there are 8 students who want to take them home, how many babies can each student have?

Each student can have _____ baby gerbils.

Check What You Learned

Problem Solving: Division Facts through 81 ÷ 9

Read the problem carefully and solve. Show your work under each question.

The marching bands from four area schools are in a large parade. Each band marches in rows with the same number of students in each row. Leo's school band has 45 members. Taro's school band has 72 members. Maya's school band has 32 members, and Barbara's school band has 63 members.

CHAPTER 2 POSTTEST

1. Maya's school band marches in 4 rows. How many band members are there in each row?

   _____ band members

2. Taro's school band marches with 9 band members in each row. How many rows does the band have? Write a division equation. Then, solve.

   _____

   _____ rows

3. Barbara's band director plans to have 7 rows. How many band members are in each row? What multiplication sentence can be used to check this division?

   _____ band members

   _____

4. Leo's school band also marches with 9 band members in each row. How many rows does the band have?

   _____ rows

Mid-Test Chapters 1–2

Divide.

	a	b	c	d	e
1.	5)25	4)16	7)21	9)81	6)18
2.	6)54	3)27	9)72	7)49	5)5
3.	3)24	4)28	9)36	2)14	1)9
4.	3)6	8)16	7)35	5)15	3)9
5.	7)42	9)45	2)2	7)63	2)6
6.	5)20	2)18	8)32	4)24	8)72
7.	1)1	8)64	6)36	5)45	2)16
8.	8)48	3)15	3)21	9)54	1)5
9.	8)24	7)28	4)36	7)14	9)9
10.	5)35	6)42	5)45	1)2	9)63

MID-TEST CHAPTERS 1-2

Mid-Test Chapters 1–2

Solve each problem. Show your work under each question.

11. A group of 7 boys cut lawns over the weekend. They made 56 dollars. Each boy will make the same amount. How much money will each boy get?

Each boy will get _____ dollars.

12. Gloria decided to make lemonade for her family. There are 8 people in her family. The pitcher will hold 24 glasses of lemonade. How many glasses can each person have? Write a division equation. Then, solve.

_____

Each person can have _____ glasses.

13. Susan, Marta, and Aisha have 5 hours to spend at the zoo. There are 40 different animals they want to see. During each hour at the zoo, how many animals should they plan to see?

They should plan to see _____ different animals each hour.

14. Write the rule for this table.

In	Out
48	8
24	4
42	7
18	3

_____

NAME _____

 Check What You Know

Dividing through 4 Digits by 1 Digit

Divide.

	a	b	c	d	e
1.	2)42	2)15	2)142	3)63	3)180
2.	5)152	3)521	8)55	7)70	4)98
3.	9)87	7)77	2)50	2)8142	3)900
4.	3)45	5)105	5)6500	8)78	3)68
5.	5)1905	6)121	7)62	7)22	2)90

NAME _____

SCORE ⬤ / 20

Dividing 2 Digits

x	1	2	3	4	5
8	8	16	24	32	40

$$\begin{array}{r} 4 \\ 8\overline{)33} \\ -32 \\ \hline 1 \end{array}$$

8×4

Subtract.

33 is between 32 and 40, so 33 ÷ 8 is between 4 and 5. The ones digit is 4.

Since 33 − 32 = 1 and 1 is less than 8, the remainder 1 is recorded like this. ⟶

$$\begin{array}{r} 4\ r\ 1 \\ 8\overline{)33} \\ -32 \\ \hline 1 \end{array}$$

Divide.

	a	b	c	d	e
1.	$5\overline{)26}$	$7\overline{)58}$	$4\overline{)31}$	$9\overline{)82}$	$6\overline{)35}$
2.	$8\overline{)66}$	$3\overline{)17}$	$2\overline{)13}$	$7\overline{)50}$	$6\overline{)40}$
3.	$9\overline{)30}$	$5\overline{)41}$	$3\overline{)10}$	$8\overline{)73}$	$7\overline{)57}$
4.	$8\overline{)20}$	$6\overline{)37}$	$9\overline{)55}$	$7\overline{)29}$	$5\overline{)47}$

Dividing 2 Digits

Divide.

	a	b	c	d	e
1.	2)36	5)76	7)79	4)96	7)93
2.	5)86	3)96	8)99	7)84	3)75
3.	6)93	6)72	8)89	7)89	9)99
4.	4)88	3)84	2)77	4)78	8)93

Division Practice

Divide.

	a	b	c	d	e
1.	$4\overline{)17}$	$3\overline{)22}$	$4\overline{)21}$	$3\overline{)29}$	$4\overline{)26}$
2.	$8\overline{)34}$	$8\overline{)27}$	$4\overline{)30}$	$7\overline{)23}$	$5\overline{)32}$
3.	$3\overline{)26}$	$5\overline{)38}$	$3\overline{)20}$	$4\overline{)37}$	$9\overline{)38}$
4.	$6\overline{)21}$	$5\overline{)42}$	$5\overline{)26}$	$4\overline{)35}$	$2\overline{)15}$
5.	$7\overline{)29}$	$9\overline{)48}$	$5\overline{)22}$	$9\overline{)28}$	$6\overline{)34}$

Division Practice

Divide.

	a	b	c	d	e
1.	$7\overline{)30}$	$8\overline{)43}$	$9\overline{)75}$	$6\overline{)26}$	$5\overline{)27}$
2.	$8\overline{)26}$	$6\overline{)52}$	$9\overline{)39}$	$4\overline{)34}$	$9\overline{)48}$
3.	$7\overline{)38}$	$3\overline{)22}$	$5\overline{)37}$	$6\overline{)38}$	$6\overline{)33}$
4.	$\overset{9\ R1}{3\overline{)26}}$	$8\overline{)58}$	$7\overline{)51}$	$9\overline{)84}$	$4\overline{)30}$
5.	$\overset{5\ R2}{4\overline{)22}}$	$9\overline{)64}$	$6\overline{)45}$	$8\overline{)66}$	$7\overline{)65}$

Division Practice

Divide.

	a	b	c	d	e
1.	$8\overline{)74}$	$5\overline{)32}$	$6\overline{)50}$	$3\overline{)20}$	$9\overline{)50}$
2.	$7\overline{)59}$	$4\overline{)38}$	$8\overline{)50}$	$4\overline{)27}$	$9\overline{)47}$
3.	$8\overline{)61}$	$7\overline{)40}$	$6\overline{)57}$	$9\overline{)82}$	$2\overline{)11}$
4.	$7\overline{)48}$	$9\overline{)73}$	$5\overline{)47}$	$6\overline{)44}$	$7\overline{)68}$
5.	$3\overline{)17}$	$8\overline{)47}$	$6\overline{)31}$	$5\overline{)43}$	$9\overline{)87}$

Division Practice

Divide.

	a	b	c	d	e
1.	3)68	3)86	2)47	5)57	8)89
2.	3)95	7)79	2)65	4)87	3)37
3.	5)59	2)87	4)45	3)64	2)83
4.	8)97	6)79	4)65	7)95	3)74
5.	5)72	2)53	7)86	3)47	6)81

Division Practice

Divide.

	a	b	c	d	e
1.	6)92	4)63	2)37	7)96	3)56
2.	5)63	8)99	4)55	6)85	5)74
3.	2)75	4)95	7)82	3)85	8)95
4.	4)75	5)82	3)77	6)89	2)57
5.	7)93	5)74	2)93	4)67	3)43

Division Practice

Divide.

	a	b	c	d	e
1.	2)63	5)75	9)97	7)88	5)56
2.	3)72	8)96	6)78	4)65	5)97
3.	2)75	4)34	6)93	8)89	2)69
4.	3)64	7)87	5)95	4)47	3)59
5.	4)59	6)71	2)49	7)99	8)97

Dividing 3 Digits

Since $100 \times 8 = 800$ and 800 is greater than 453, there is no hundreds digit.

$$8 \overline{)453}$$

x	10	20	30	40	50	60
8	80	160	240	320	400	480

453 is between 400 and 480. $453 \div 8$ is between 50 and 60. The tens digit is 5.

$$\begin{array}{r} 5 \\ 8 \overline{)453} \\ -40 \quad 8 \times 5 = 40 \\ \hline 53 \quad \text{Subtract} \end{array}$$

x	1	2	3	4	5	6	7
8	8	16	24	32	40	48	56

53 is between 48 and 56. $53 \div 8$ is between 6 and 7. The ones digit is 6.

$$\begin{array}{r} 56 \text{ r } 5 \\ 8 \overline{)453} \\ -40 \quad 8 \times 6 = 48 \\ \hline 53 \quad \text{Subtract} \\ -48 \\ \hline 5 \quad \text{Remainder} \end{array}$$

Divide.

	a	b	c	d	e
1.	$8 \overline{)720}$	$4 \overline{)372}$	$9 \overline{)372}$	$4 \overline{)173}$	$2 \overline{)150}$
2.	$6 \overline{)552}$	$3 \overline{)139}$	$4 \overline{)248}$	$9 \overline{)890}$	$5 \overline{)105}$
3.	$9 \overline{)780}$	$5 \overline{)225}$	$9 \overline{)813}$	$7 \overline{)511}$	$3 \overline{)110}$

Dividing 3 Digits

Divide.

	a	b	c	d	e
1.	$5\overline{)546}$	$4\overline{)762}$	$3\overline{)472}$	$6\overline{)687}$	$8\overline{)994}$
2.	$3\overline{)933}$	$4\overline{)456}$	$7\overline{)806}$	$2\overline{)451}$	$5\overline{)750}$
3.	$9\overline{)936}$	$3\overline{)768}$	$9\overline{)915}$	$4\overline{)848}$	$6\overline{)762}$
4.	$2\overline{)835}$	$2\overline{)352}$	$7\overline{)766}$	$4\overline{)506}$	$2\overline{)287}$

Division Practice

Divide.

	a	b	c	d	e
1.	6)773	2)898	4)566	6)781	3)972
2.	2)317	4)732	9)989	7)897	2)394
3.	5)529	8)897	3)676	2)348	6)930
4.	3)784	5)788	3)481	5)558	2)610
5.	3)324	5)953	6)868	3)975	6)720

Division Practice

Divide.

	a	b	c	d	e
1.	$3\overline{)225}$	$6\overline{)324}$	$9\overline{)288}$	$2\overline{)138}$	$7\overline{)455}$
2.	$4\overline{)216}$	$8\overline{)504}$	$5\overline{)270}$	$3\overline{)171}$	$6\overline{)378}$
3.	$9\overline{)855}$	$2\overline{)194}$	$7\overline{)385}$	$4\overline{)304}$	$5\overline{)435}$
4.	$3\overline{)201}$	$6\overline{)348}$	$8\overline{)744}$	$2\overline{)154}$	$9\overline{)306}$
5.	$4\overline{)224}$	$7\overline{)644}$	$5\overline{)475}$	$3\overline{)282}$	$6\overline{)588}$

Division Practice

Divide.

	a	b	c	d	e
1.	2)155	4)358	6)273	8)428	9)399
2.	3)296	5)291	7)549	2)173	5)439
3.	9)758	6)392	7)279	3)209	4)231
4.	8)699	2)119	6)507	5)197	9)489
5.	3)173	7)408	6)237	5)338	4)314

Division Practice

Divide.

	a	b	c	d	e
1.	8)532	4)269	6)562	2)179	9)659
2.	3)119	7)439	5)484	4)155	9)587
3.	8)757	2)157	3)143	6)338	2)193
4.	7)331	9)291	8)202	4)383	3)224
5.	5)374	6)537	9)867	2)135	6)446

Division Practice

Divide.

	a	b	c	d	e
1.	2)4 3 2	4)9 2 4	6)7 2 6	5)5 7 5	3)4 5 6
2.	7)7 8 4	9)9 9 9	8)8 9 6	4)8 4 8	2)9 5 2
3.	5)7 1 5	3)9 4 2	6)7 8 6	5)7 6 5	4)9 3 2
4.	3)7 5 9	2)7 2 6	5)5 8 5	7)7 8 4	2)5 4 8
5.	6)9 7 2	4)9 6 8	2)7 4 6	8)8 9 6	4)8 5 6

Division Practice

Divide.

	a	b	c	d	e
1.	2)437	6)739	4)979	5)994	3)596
2.	8)899	7)804	6)879	5)734	2)753
3.	4)595	3)748	7)978	6)887	4)759
4.	2)537	5)687	8)897	4)635	3)836
5.	6)689	2)379	5)748	8)907	6)987

SCORE ⬭ / 25

Division Practice

Divide.

	a	b	c	d	e
1.	3)746	7)796	5)893	4)943	6)676
2.	8)978	2)337	7)957	3)446	4)538
3.	6)759	5)684	8)894	2)487	3)953
4.	6)945	4)629	7)879	5)947	2)951
5.	4)739	3)647	6)857	2)859	4)938

Chapter 3
Dividing through 4 Digits by 1 Digit

Division Practice

Divide.

	a	b	c	d	e
1.	$6\overline{)65}$	$9\overline{)94}$	$3\overline{)925}$	$7\overline{)564}$	$4\overline{)823}$
2.	$5\overline{)253}$	$8\overline{)865}$	$2\overline{)841}$	$7\overline{)75}$	$6\overline{)364}$
3.	$4\overline{)414}$	$5\overline{)254}$	$8\overline{)327}$	$3\overline{)623}$	$2\overline{)461}$
4.	$7\overline{)423}$	$6\overline{)627}$	$5\overline{)529}$	$4\overline{)842}$	$3\overline{)961}$
5.	$8\overline{)325}$	$7\overline{)738}$	$6\overline{)423}$	$2\overline{)241}$	$5\overline{)539}$

Dividing 4 Digits

$8 \div 4 = 2$
$4 \times 2 = 8$

$9 \div 4 = 2$
remainder 1

$11 \div 4 = 2$
remainder 3

$37 \div 4 = 9$
remainder 1

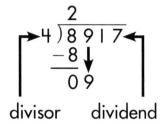

$$\begin{array}{r} 2 \\ 4\overline{)8\,9\,1\,7} \\ -8 \\ \hline 0\,9 \end{array}$$

divisor   dividend

$$\begin{array}{r} 2\,2 \\ 4\overline{)8\,9\,1\,7} \\ -8 \\ \hline 0\,9 \\ -8 \\ \hline 1\,1 \end{array}$$

$$\begin{array}{r} 2\,2\,2 \\ 4\overline{)8\,9\,1\,7} \\ -8 \\ \hline 0\,9 \\ -8 \\ \hline 1\,1 \\ -8 \\ \hline 3\,7 \end{array}$$

$$\begin{array}{r} 2\,2\,2\,9 \\ 4\overline{)8\,9\,1\,7} \\ -8 \\ \hline 0\,9 \\ -8 \\ \hline 1\,1 \\ -8 \\ \hline 3\,7 \\ -3\,6 \\ \hline 1 \end{array}$$ ← quotient

← remainder

Divide.

	a	b	c	d
1.	$3\overline{)4650}$	$6\overline{)3925}$	$8\overline{)1487}$	$2\overline{)9234}$
2.	$7\overline{)6496}$	$4\overline{)8568}$	$7\overline{)1426}$	$3\overline{)3746}$
3.	$5\overline{)8503}$	$9\overline{)6292}$	$4\overline{)3166}$	$2\overline{)2317}$

Division Practice

Divide.

	a	b	c	d
1.	$2\overline{)3486}$	$4\overline{)8572}$	$6\overline{)3764}$	$5\overline{)5328}$
2.	$3\overline{)2874}$	$2\overline{)8497}$	$7\overline{)8598}$	$2\overline{)8040}$
3.	$4\overline{)2988}$	$6\overline{)8149}$	$7\overline{)5001}$	$3\overline{)6238}$
4.	$5\overline{)7384}$	$8\overline{)4376}$	$2\overline{)4811}$	$4\overline{)1583}$
5.	$6\overline{)7391}$	$3\overline{)6943}$	$7\overline{)4795}$	$5\overline{)5237}$

Division Practice

Divide.

	a	b	c	d
1.	8)3216	4)1272	7)1502	3)296
2.	6)4811	9)788	5)554	8)1143
3.	4)362	3)1553	6)5554	7)487
4.	2)1694	4)1550	9)7155	5)2093
5.	7)4778	3)316	6)483	4)515

Division Practice

Divide.

	a	b	c	d
1.	5)2013	8)1886	9)2591	7)3330
2.	2)219	3)632	5)1835	8)567
3.	6)6150	4)1278	5)4250	2)819
4.	9)1123	7)2273	8)1126	3)8693
5.	4)2086	6)2464	9)1088	8)9198

NAME _____

SCORE ⬭ /24

Division and Place Value

Use patterns of place value to help determine the divisor.

If, $8 \div \underline{\textbf{2}} = 4$

Then, using place value, you can find the divisor in greater numbers.

$80 \div \underline{\textbf{2}} = 40 \quad \longrightarrow \quad 80 \div 2 = 40$

$800 \div \underline{\textbf{2}} = 400 \quad \longrightarrow \quad 800 \div 2 = 400$

$8000 \div \underline{\textbf{2}} = 4000 \quad \longrightarrow \quad 8000 \div 2 = 4000$

Fill in the missing numbers.

a **b**

1. $7 \div \underline{\quad} = 1$ $6 \div \underline{\quad} = 2$

   $70 \div \underline{\quad} = 10$ $60 \div \underline{\quad} = 20$

   $700 \div \underline{\quad} = 100$ $600 \div \underline{\quad} = 200$

   $7000 \div \underline{\quad} = 1000$ $6000 \div \underline{\quad} = 2000$

2. $12 \div \underline{\quad} = 3$ $10 \div \underline{\quad} = 2$

   $120 \div \underline{\quad} = 30$ $100 \div \underline{\quad} = 20$

   $1200 \div \underline{\quad} = 300$ $1000 \div \underline{\quad} = 200$

   $12000 \div \underline{\quad} = 3000$ $10000 \div \underline{\quad} = 2000$

3. $9 \div \underline{\quad} = 3$ $5 \div \underline{\quad} = 1$

   $90 \div \underline{\quad} = 30$ $50 \div \underline{\quad} = 10$

   $900 \div \underline{\quad} = 300$ $500 \div \underline{\quad} = 100$

   $9000 \div \underline{\quad} = 3000$ $5000 \div \underline{\quad} = 1000$

Spectrum Division
Grade 4
62

Chapter 3
Dividing through 4 Digits by 1 Digit

Division and Place Value

Divide.

	a	b	c	d
1.	3)300	2)6000	2)20	4)800
2.	10)400	300)9000	40)1200	10)100
3.	7)140	2)80	700)1400	40)120
4.	3)900	600)1800	2000)10000	30)600
5.	8)1600	20)140	90)180	30)90

Division Practice

Divide.

	a	**b**	**c**	**d**
1.	3)45	9)72	2)34	4)76
2.	6)493	3)873	7)875	5)987
3.	7)2598	2)5282	6)5631	4)9637
4.	6)9832	8)5000	5)7004	7)5111
5.	5)85	8)800	5)2515	8)9840

Estimating Quotients

$$7\overline{)24}$$

$$\begin{array}{r} 3 \\ 7\overline{)21} \\ -21 \\ \hline 0 \end{array}$$

Think of what you can round the dividend (24) to so that it is easy to mentally divide by the divisor (7). The quotient is 3.

$$5\overline{)378}$$

quotient ⟶
$$\begin{array}{r} 76 \\ 5\overline{)380} \\ -35 \\ \hline 30 \\ -30 \\ \hline 0 \end{array}$$

Think of what you can round the dividend (378) to so that it is easy to mentally divide by the divisor (5).

Divide.

	a	b	c	d
1.	$3\overline{)16}$	$7\overline{)36}$	$3\overline{)74}$	$4\overline{)83}$
2.	$4\overline{)27}$	$6\overline{)217}$	$8\overline{)481}$	$7\overline{)764}$
3.	$9\overline{)362}$	$2\overline{)563}$	$4\overline{)1378}$	$3\overline{)4269}$
4.	$8\overline{)2448}$	$5\overline{)9216}$	$9\overline{)3502}$	$5\overline{)7358}$

Check What You Learned

Dividing through 4 Digits by 1 Digit

Divide.

	a	b	c	d	e
1.	2)32	3)9000	3)49	8)97	2)178
2.	4)6121	6)798	5)557	6)636	8)889
3.	2)96	3)87	8)1600	3)42	7)31
4.	8)75	2)19	8)43	9)89	3)60
5.	3)603	5)100	6)762	7)37	2)48

Check What You Know

Problem Solving: Dividing through 4 Digits by 1 Digit

Read the problem carefully and solve. Show your work under each question.

A bookstore needs to pack books in boxes to ship. Each box can only hold one type of book. Each type of book must be divided evenly between the boxes. There are 167 nonfiction books and 89 mystery books. There are 35 picture books and 108 fiction books.

---

1. If the mystery books are packed in 6 boxes, how many mystery books will be in each box? How many mystery books will be left over?

_____ mystery books

_____ books left over

2. If 8 picture books can fit into each box, how many boxes can they fill? How many total boxes will the store need to ship all of the picture books? Explain your answer.

_____ full boxes

_____ total number of boxes needed

_____

3. The bookstore plans to use 7 boxes to ship the nonfiction books. How many nonfiction books will fit in each box? How many will be left over?

_____ nonfiction books

_____ books left over

4. The store only has 3 boxes left to ship all the fiction books. Will all the fiction books fit or will there be some left over? Explain your answer.

_____

Dividing 2 Digits

Read the problem carefully and solve. Show your work under each question.

Two different soccer teams need to carpool to the next game. There are 16 players on Molly's team. Each car on Molly's team can hold 5 players. There are 18 players on Lian's team. Each car on Lian's team can hold 4 players. Lian's team has 4 cars.

Helpful Hint

If a number does not divide into another number evenly, there will be a **remainder** (r).

$$\begin{array}{r} 3 \ \text{r} \ 1 \\ 7\overline{)22} \\ -21 \\ \hline 1 \end{array}$$

1. How many cars can Molly's team fill? How many players will be left over?

_____ full cars

_____ player left

2. How many cars will Molly's team need to take all the players to the game? Explain your answer.

_____ cars

_____

3. Does Lian's team have enough cars to take all their players to the game? If not, how many players still need a ride?

_____

Dividing 3 Digits

Read the problem carefully and solve. Show your work under each question.

Natalia and Manuel have a large stamp collection. They organize their stamps into one album. They put the same number of each type of stamp on a page. Natalia and Manuel have 274 animal stamps, 108 sports stamps, 148 flower stamps, and 324 stamps of famous people and events.

> **Helpful Hint**
>
> Remember to write the first digit of the quotient in the correct spot.
>
> $$7\overline{)434}^{62}$$
>
> Since $100 \times 7 = 700$ and 700 is greater than 437, there is no hundreds digit in the quotient.

1. Natalia wants to use 8 pages of the album for the animal stamps. How many animal stamps will be on each page? How many animal stamps will be left over?

   _____ stamps on a page

   _____ stamps left over

2. Manuel decides to use 4 pages of the album for sports stamps. How many sports stamps will be on each page? How many sports stamps will be left over?

   _____ stamps on a page

   _____ stamps left over

Dividing 4 Digits

Read the problem carefully and solve. Show your work under each question.

Middle City Hardware is having a big sale. The staff workers are putting tools and other items in groups for the sale.

---

1. Josie's boss gives her 3,258 bolts. Her boss says to put the bolts in bags of 9 bolts each. How many full bags of bolts will she have?

_____ bags

2. Chad has 1,137 screwdrivers. Chad puts them in sets of 4. How many screwdrivers will be left over when he is finished?

_____ left over

3. Special sale items are worth $7,527 in all. The sale will last for 3 days. How much money will the store make per day if the sales are equal each day?

_____

SCORE ◯ / 3

Division and Place Value

Solve each problem. Show your work under each question.

1. The cross-country team runs 70 miles a week. If they stop for a break every 7 miles, how many breaks do they take each week?

They take _____ breaks each week.

2. The pool's lap lane is 800 feet long. If a swimmer splits this length into 4 equal sections, how many feet will each section be?

Each section will be _____ feet.

3. The garden show is moving into a bigger area. The new area has 1,200 square feet of space for displays. There are 300 different displays, and each display will need the same amount of space. How many square feet does each display get?

Each display gets _____ square feet of space.

Division Practice

Solve each problem. Show your work under each question.

1. A boys' club picked up litter in the park. They collected 913 bags of litter. If each boy collected about the same amount, about how many bags did the 7 boys collect? How many extra bags were collected?

   Each boy picked up about _____ bags.

   There were _____ extra bags collected.

2. The school supply store received a shipment of 730 pens. If the pens are packed in 5 boxes, how many pens are in each box?

   There are _____ pens in each box.

3. Taylor needs 612 more dollars to buy a plane ticket to visit his cousin in Australia. If he saves 9 dollars a day, how soon can he go to Australia?

   He will have the rest of the money in _____ days.

Division Practice

Solve each problem. Show your work under each question.

1. The school office received 22 computers. If there are 9 classrooms receiving the computers, how many computers will go to each classroom? How many computers will be left?

Each classroom will receive _____ computers.

There will be _____ extra computers.

2. There are 60 summer jobs for lifeguards at the city pools. There will be 3 lifeguards at each city pool. How many city pools are there?

There are _____ city pools.

3. At the Hot Dog Shack, customers bought 27 hot dogs on Saturday. There were only 9 customers. How many hot dogs did each customer buy?

Each customer bought _____ hot dogs.

Division Practice

Solve each problem. Show your work under each question.

1. The school spirit club baked cakes for a charity event. There were 75 different types of cakes. Each baker baked the same number of cakes. If there were 5 bakers, how many cakes did each baker make?

Each baker made _____ cakes.

2. The Fish Shop is open 72 hours a week. The shop is open 6 days a week and the same number of hours each day. How many hours each day is the shop open?

The shop is open _____ hours a day.

3. The glee club needs to sell 382 tickets to win a trip. If there are 8 members who want to go on the trip, how many tickets does each member need to sell? How many extra tickets will be left?

Each member needs to sell _____ tickets.

There will be _____ extra tickets.

Estimating Quotients

Read the problem carefully and solve. Show your work under each question.

The Quick Haul Trucking Company makes local deliveries. The shipping manager divides all of the boxes into various shipments. Sometimes, the manager makes estimates for the shipments.

Helpful Hint

To estimate a quotient, round the dividend into a number that is easily divided by the divisor.

To estimate the quotient of 45 divided by 7, first round 45 into 42. Then, a good estimate of the quotient is 6.

1. Quick Haul delivers 133 boxes to 3 stores. Each store gets about the same number of boxes. Estimate the number of boxes going to each store.

   About _____ boxes

2. Quick Haul trucks can carry 9 boxes of one size. There is a shipment of 83 boxes to deliver. Estimate the number of truckloads for the shipment.

   About _____ truckloads

3. Quick Haul delivers 103 lamps to 7 stores. If each store gets about the same number of lamps, about how many lamps will each store get?

   About _____ lamps

Check What You Learned

Problem Solving: Dividing through 4 Digits by 1 Digit

Read the problem carefully and solve. Show your work under each question.

Kenesha, Shawna, and Jake have postcard collections. They each plan to put their postcards into scrapbooks to organize them. Kenesha has 144 postcards, Shawna has 59 postcards, and Jake has 98 postcards.

CHAPTER 4 POSTTEST

1. Shawna only wants to use 9 pages of her scrapbook. How many postcards should she put on each page? How many will be left over?

   _____ postcards

   _____ postcards left over

2. Jake can fit 4 postcards on each page of his scrapbook. How many pages can he fill with his postcards? If he wants to put all of his postcards in the scrapbook, how many total pages will he need to use?

   _____ full pages

   _____ total pages needed

3. Kenesha plans to put 8 postcards on each page of her scrapbook. How many pages can she fill? How many postcards will be left over?

   _____ pages

   _____ postcards left over

4. Kenesha and Shawna decide to combine their postcard collections to make a collage. Each girl will get half of the total number of postcards. How many postcards will each girl get to use in the collage? How many will be left over?

   _____ postcards

   _____ postcard(s) left over

Final Test Chapters 1–4

Divide.

	a	b	c	d	e
1.	$9\overline{)81}$	$7\overline{)56}$	$8\overline{)48}$	$8\overline{)160}$	$7\overline{)42}$
2.	$8\overline{)24}$	$5\overline{)35}$	$7\overline{)28}$	$6\overline{)54}$	$9\overline{)72}$
3.	$3\overline{)330}$	$2\overline{)642}$	$7\overline{)721}$	$4\overline{)6484}$	$8\overline{)864}$
4.	$8\overline{)724}$	$7\overline{)639}$	$5\overline{)1000}$	$6\overline{)247}$	$2\overline{)876}$
5.	$9\overline{)8458}$	$7\overline{)807}$	$6\overline{)684}$	$3\overline{)949}$	$4\overline{)2713}$
6.	$9\overline{)908}$	$2\overline{)510}$	$4\overline{)648}$	$8\overline{)7888}$	$6\overline{)1800}$

Final Test Chapters 1–4

Divide.

	a	b	c	d	e
7.	9⟌81	7⟌56	8⟌48	8⟌160	7⟌42
8.	8⟌24	5⟌35	7⟌28	6⟌54	9⟌72
9.	3⟌330	2⟌642	7⟌721	4⟌6484	8⟌864
10.	8⟌724	7⟌639	5⟌1000	6⟌247	2⟌876

Fill in the missing numbers.

a

b

11.
$9 \div \_\_\_\_ = 1$
$90 \div \_\_\_\_ = 10$
$900 \div \_\_\_\_ = 100$
$9000 \div \_\_\_\_ = 1000$

$4 \div \_\_\_\_ = 2$
$40 \div \_\_\_\_ = 20$
$400 \div \_\_\_\_ = 200$
$4000 \div \_\_\_\_ = 2000$

12.
$16 \div \_\_\_\_ = 4$
$160 \div \_\_\_\_ = 40$
$1600 \div \_\_\_\_ = 400$
$16000 \div \_\_\_\_ = 4000$

$15 \div \_\_\_\_ = 5$
$1500 \div \_\_\_\_ = 500$
$15000 \div \_\_\_\_ = 5000$
$150000 \div \_\_\_\_ = 50000$

Final Test Chapters 1–4

Divide.

	a	b	c	d	e
13.	8)87	5)53	4)842	7)426	3)92
14.	6)484	8)839	2)615	9)98	6)543
15.	7)73	4)483	3)272	5)517	7)634
16.	2)815	6)364	4)323	8)726	3)631

Find the rule and complete each table.

a			b			c	

17.

In	Out
32	8
28	
8	2
36	
40	

In	Out
35	7
45	
10	2
30	
5	

In	Out
56	
16	2
40	
64	
72	9

_____   _____   _____

Final Test Chapters 1–4

Solve each problem. Show your work under each question.

18. A restaurant has 245 seats with 5 seats at each table. How many tables does the restaurant have?

   The restaurant has _____ tables.

19. Homer buys 3 newspapers every week. If Homer has 627 newspapers, how many weeks has he been buying them?

   He has been buying newspapers for _____ weeks.

20. A group of 30 children started a lawn mowing company at the beginning of the summer. At the end of the summer, the company had mowed 600 lawns. How many lawns did each child mow if each mowed an equal number?

   Each child mowed _____ lawns.

21. The Wilkinson family drove 1,374 miles in 9 days. How many miles did the Wilkinsons drive each day if they drove the same amount? How many more miles did they drive on the last day?

   The Wilkinson family drove _____ miles each day.

   They drove _____ extra miles on the last day.

Final Test Chapters 1–4

Solve each problem. Show your work under each question.

22. Ms. Garrett had 40 guests at her birthday party. She cut her cake into 88 slices. Each guest ate 2 pieces of cake. How many slices were left?

There were _____ slices left.

23. Lucy babysits for 2 families. She works the same number of hours each month for each family. If she worked 76 hours last month, how many hours did she work for each family?

She worked _____ hours for each family.

24. Tom and Jose enjoy playing video games. Together, they play 10 hours a week. If they play 5 days a week for the same number of hours each day, how many hours do they both play together?

They play together _____ hours a day.

25. At the basketball tournament, 28 people signed up to play. If there were 4 teams, how many players were on a team? Write a division equation. Then, solve.

_____

There were _____ players on each team.

Final Test Chapters 1–4

Solve each problem. Show your work under each question.

26. Howard Jackson scored 158 points this season playing basketball. He played in 7 games and scored about the same number of points in each game. About how many points did he score in each game?

He scored about _____ points in each game.

27. Miss Gomez drove 256 miles in 4 hours. She drove the same number of miles each hour. How many miles did she drive in 1 hour?

She drove _____ miles in 1 hour.

28. In the past 6 weeks, Jackson worked on 738 computers. Each week, he worked on the same number of computers. How many computers did he work on every week?

He worked on _____ computers every week.

29. At baseball practice, 1,325 pitches were thrown to the players. If 5 players got the same number of pitches, how many pitches did each player get?

Each player got _____ pitches.

Scoring Record for Pretests, Posttests, Mid-Test, and Final Test

Pretests, Posttests, Mid-Test, and Final Test	Your Score	Performance			
		Excellent	Very Good	Fair	Needs Improvement
Chapter 1 Pretest	____ of 50	48–50	41–47	30–40	29 or fewer
Chapter 1 Posttest	____ of 50	48–50	41–47	30–40	29 or fewer
Chapter 2 Pretest	____ of 5	5	4	3	2 or fewer
Chapter 2 Posttest	____ of 5	5	4	3	2 or fewer
Chapter 3 Pretest	____ of 25	24–25	20–23	15–19	14 or fewer
Chapter 3 Posttest	____ of 25	24–24	20–23	15–19	14 or fewer
Chapter 4 Pretest	____ of 8	7	6	5	4 or fewer
Chapter 4 Posttest	____ of 8	7	6	5	4 or fewer
Mid-Test	____ of 55	52–55	44–51	33–43	32 or fewer
Final Test	____ of 109	104–109	88–103	66–87	65 or fewer

Record your test score in the Your Score column. See where your score falls in the Performance columns. Your score is based on the total number of required responses. If your score is fair or needs improvement, review the chapter material.

Answer Key

Check What You Know
Division Facts through 81 ÷ 9
CHAPTER 1 PRETEST

Divide.

	a	b	c	d	e
1.	3)15 = 5	7)49 = 7	9)27 = 3	5)45 = 9	7)21 = 3
2.	3)18 = 6	7)42 = 6	9)81 = 9	7)56 = 8	6)30 = 5
3.	4)36 = 9	4)16 = 4	5)40 = 8	2)10 = 5	4)36 = 9
4.	9)18 = 2	5)35 = 7	7)28 = 4	2)6 = 3	4)24 = 6
5.	5)15 = 3	3)21 = 7	9)54 = 6	4)8 = 2	2)14 = 7
6.	6)36 = 6	6)48 = 8	8)32 = 4	3)24 = 8	3)9 = 3
7.	8)72 = 9	8)64 = 8	5)25 = 5	9)9 = 1	3)0 = 0
8.	5)35 = 7	5)20 = 4	4)36 = 9	8)56 = 7	2)12 = 6
9.	2)18 = 9	3)27 = 9	4)28 = 7	2)2 = 1	2)8 = 4
10.	3)15 = 5	9)63 = 7	6)48 = 8	7)14 = 2	9)27 = 3

Spectrum Division
Grade 4
Chapter 1
Division Facts through 81 ÷ 9
5

NAME _____ SCORE __ / 18

Dividing through 45 ÷ 5

divisor → 5)45 ← dividend, quotient 9

To check your answer, do the inverse operation.
If 45 ÷ 5 = 9, then 5 × 9 = 45 must be true.

Using the division table, find 45 in the 5 column. The quotient is named at the beginning of the row.

Divide.

	a	b	c	d	e
1.	5)35 = 7	4)16 = 4	4)36 = 9	3)18 = 6	5)25 = 5
2.	2)18 = 9	3)18 = 6	3)27 = 9	3)12 = 4	5)20 = 4
3.	5)45 = 9	3)15 = 5	5)30 = 6	4)32 = 8	2)8 = 4

Complete the following.

	a	b	c
4.	5 ×3 = 15 so 3)15 = 5	4 ×7 = 28 so 7)28 = 4	3 ×4 = 12 so 4)12 = 3

Spectrum Division
Grade 4
Chapter 1
Division Facts through 81 ÷ 9
6

NAME _____ SCORE __ / 23

Dividing through 45 ÷ 5

Divide.

	a	b	c	d	e
1.	3)21 = 7	2)10 = 5	2)16 = 8	2)12 = 6	9)45 = 5
2.	5)35 = 7	2)18 = 9	5)40 = 8	5)30 = 6	4)24 = 6
3.	3)24 = 8	4)20 = 5	3)9 = 3	4)12 = 3	2)14 = 7
4.	4)4 = 1	5)15 = 3	5)10 = 2	4)0 = 0	3)6 = 2

Complete the following.

	a	b	c
5.	4 ×6 = 24 so 6)24 = 4	3 ×8 = 24 so 8)24 = 3	5 ×6 = 30 so 6)30 = 5

Spectrum Division
Grade 4
Chapter 1
Division Facts through 81 ÷ 9
7

NAME _____ SCORE __ / 18

Dividing through 63 ÷ 7

divisor → 7)63 ← dividend, quotient 9

To check your answer, do the inverse operation.
If 63 ÷ 7 = 9, then 7 × 9 = 63 must be true.

Using the division table, find 63 in the 7 column. The quotient is named at the end of the row.

Divide.

	a	b	c	d	e
1.	7)49 = 7	5)45 = 9	6)36 = 6	3)24 = 8	3)27 = 9
2.	2)18 = 9	4)24 = 6	6)48 = 8	4)32 = 8	5)45 = 9
3.	5)40 = 8	2)12 = 6	6)6 = 1	7)56 = 8	7)0 = 0

Complete the following.

	a	b	c
4.	7 ×6 = 42 so 7)42 = 6	5 ×9 = 45 so 9)45 = 5	8 ×7 = 56 so 7)56 = 8

Spectrum Division
Grade 4
Chapter 1
Division Facts through 81 ÷ 9
8

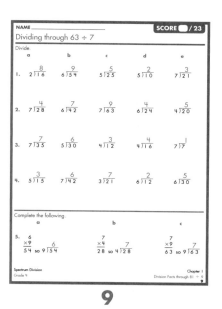

NAME _____ SCORE __ / 23

Dividing through 63 ÷ 7

Divide.

	a	b	c	d	e
1.	2)16 = 8	6)54 = 9	5)25 = 5	5)10 = 2	7)21 = 3
2.	7)28 = 4	6)42 = 7	7)63 = 9	6)24 = 4	4)20 = 5
3.	7)35 = 5	5)30 = 6	4)12 = 3	4)16 = 4	7)7 = 1
4.	5)15 = 3	7)42 = 6	3)21 = 7	6)12 = 2	6)30 = 5

Complete the following.

	a	b	c
5.	9 ×6 = 54 so 9)54 = 6	4 ×7 = 28 so 4)28 = 7	9 ×7 = 63 so 9)63 = 7

Spectrum Division
Grade 4
Chapter 1
Division Facts through 81 ÷ 9
9

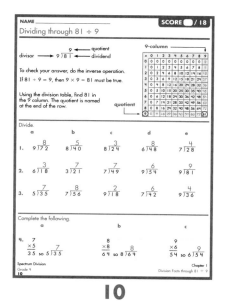

NAME _____ SCORE __ / 18

Dividing through 81 ÷ 9

divisor → 9)81 ← dividend, quotient 9

To check your answer, do the inverse operation.
If 81 ÷ 9 = 9, then 9 × 9 = 81 must be true.

Using the division table, find 81 in the 9 column. The quotient is named at the end of the row.

Divide.

	a	b	c	d	e
1.	9)72 = 8	8)40 = 5	8)24 = 3	6)48 = 8	7)28 = 4
2.	6)18 = 3	3)21 = 7	7)49 = 7	9)54 = 6	9)81 = 9
3.	5)35 = 7	7)56 = 8	9)18 = 2	7)42 = 6	9)36 = 4

Complete the following.

	a	b	c
4.	7 ×5 = 35 so 5)35 = 7	8 ×8 = 64 so 8)64 = 8	9 ×6 = 54 so 6)54 = 9

Spectrum Division
Grade 4
Chapter 1
Division Facts through 81 ÷ 9
10

11

Dividing through 81 ÷ 9

Divide.

	a	b	c	d	e
1.	7)42 = 6	5)45 = 9	8)32 = 4	7)63 = 9	8)64 = 8
2.	6)36 = 6	4)32 = 8	7)28 = 4	9)0 = 0	4)28 = 7
3.	9)45 = 5	5)30 = 6	4)12 = 3	5)25 = 5	7)14 = 2
4.	9)9 = 1	8)40 = 5	8)48 = 6	6)42 = 7	3)27 = 9

Complete the following.

	a	b	c
5.	9 ×4 = 36 so 4)36 = 9	7 ×9 = 63 so 9)63 = 7	6 ×8 = 48 so 8)48 = 6

Spectrum Division
Grade 4
Chapter 1 — Division Facts through 81 ÷ 9

12

Division Practice

Divide.

	a	b	c	d	e
1.	8)56 = 7	6)24 = 4	2)18 = 9	5)35 = 7	7)42 = 6
2.	6)48 = 8	6)30 = 5	8)72 = 9	6)36 = 6	9)81 = 9
3.	9)54 = 6	3)21 = 7	7)28 = 4	3)18 = 6	2)18 = 9
4.	5)45 = 9	9)36 = 4	6)42 = 7	8)64 = 8	7)63 = 9
5.	3)24 = 8	9)27 = 3	5)20 = 4	7)49 = 7	5)25 = 5

Spectrum Division
Grade 4
Chapter 1 — Division Facts through 81 ÷ 9

13

Division Practice

Divide.

	a	b	c	d	e
1.	3)9 = 3	2)4 = 2	3)6 = 2	4)8 = 2	1)7 = 7
2.	3)0 = 0	2)10 = 5	7)14 = 2	2)6 = 3	3)54 = 18
3.	1)5 = 5	3)12 = 4	6)12 = 2	2)2 = 1	5)10 = 2
4.	5)25 = 5	4)16 = 4	3)15 = 5	8)72 = 9	2)2 = 1

Find the rule and complete each table.

5.

a In	Out
21	3
35	5
63	9
49	7
14	2

divide by 7

b In	Out
12	6
10	5
14	7
18	9
22	

divide by 2

c In	Out
81	9
36	4
54	6
72	8
9	

divide by 9

Spectrum Division
Grade 4
Chapter 1 — Division Facts through 81 ÷ 9

14

Division Practice

Divide.

	a	b	c	d	e
1.	4)28 = 7	4)4 = 1	2)18 = 9	6)18 = 3	9)63 = 7
2.	7)63 = 9	3)27 = 9	4)32 = 8	8)64 = 8	8)48 = 6
3.	4)24 = 6	9)72 = 8	8)32 = 4	5)20 = 4	9)45 = 5
4.	6)24 = 4	7)49 = 7	9)81 = 9	5)30 = 6	3)21 = 7
5.	8)16 = 2	2)8 = 4	7)28 = 4	7)42 = 6	6)48 = 8

Spectrum Division
Grade 4
Chapter 1 — Division Facts through 81 ÷ 9

15

Division Practice

Divide.

	a	b	c	d	e
1.	5)30 = 6	7)21 = 3	4)28 = 7	9)63 = 7	5)35 = 7
2.	1)9 = 9	4)24 = 6	8)32 = 4	6)36 = 6	2)14 = 7
3.	7)56 = 8	4)36 = 9	9)27 = 3	6)42 = 7	8)8 = 1
4.	3)24 = 8	7)63 = 9	9)54 = 6	3)27 = 9	1)7 = 7
5.	8)24 = 3	2)16 = 8	7)42 = 6	6)54 = 9	8)56 = 7

Spectrum Division
Grade 4
Chapter 1 — Division Facts through 81 ÷ 9

16

Division Practice

Divide.

	a	b	c	d	e
1.	3)15 = 5	8)40 = 5	3)21 = 7	9)36 = 4	4)20 = 5
2.	8)32 = 4	9)9 = 1	5)35 = 7	9)81 = 9	6)36 = 6
3.	4)32 = 8	8)64 = 8	1)4 = 4	7)42 = 6	7)28 = 4
4.	6)30 = 5	3)24 = 8	6)48 = 8	9)54 = 6	3)18 = 6
5.	8)72 = 9	6)24 = 4	8)56 = 7	7)35 = 5	4)28 = 7

Spectrum Division
Grade 4
Chapter 1 — Division Facts through 81 ÷ 9

Spectrum Division
Grade 4

Answer Key

Answer Key

Page 17

Division Practice — SCORE /29

Divide.

	a	b	c	d	e
1.	6)48 = 8	7)28 = 4	7)42 = 6	8)56 = 7	6)24 = 4
2.	5)35 = 7	8)64 = 8	6)30 = 5	9)63 = 7	7)49 = 7
3.	8)40 = 5	9)54 = 6	4)32 = 8	5)45 = 9	7)56 = 8
4.	4)36 = 9	5)30 = 6	7)63 = 9	8)72 = 9	7)35 = 5

Find the rule and complete each table.

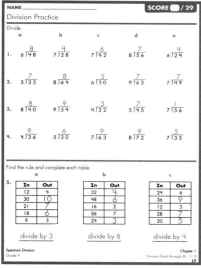

5.

a — divide by 3

In	Out
12	4
30	10
21	7
18	6
9	3

b — divide by 8

In	Out
32	4
48	6
16	2
56	7
24	3

c — divide by 4

In	Out
24	6
36	9
12	3
28	7
20	5

Spectrum Division, Grade 4 — Chapter 1, Division Facts through 81 ÷ 9 — 17

Page 18

Division Practice — SCORE /25

Divide.

	a	b	c	d	e
1.	6)48 = 8	4)32 = 8	6)36 = 6	7)42 = 6	7)28 = 4
2.	9)45 = 5	8)56 = 7	6)30 = 5	9)54 = 6	7)49 = 7
3.	5)35 = 7	6)24 = 4	9)36 = 4	8)40 = 5	9)63 = 7
4.	7)21 = 3	6)54 = 9	4)20 = 5	8)32 = 4	7)56 = 8
5.	3)21 = 7	5)40 = 8	5)20 = 4	5)45 = 9	7)35 = 5

Spectrum Division, Grade 4 — Chapter 1, Division Facts through 81 ÷ 9 — 18

Page 19

Division Practice — SCORE /25

Divide.

	a	b	c	d	e
1.	4)12 = 3	3)15 = 5	2)18 = 9	6)24 = 4	3)21 = 7
2.	5)25 = 5	4)16 = 4	5)20 = 4	7)14 = 2	8)8 = 1
3.	4)32 = 8	6)30 = 5	3)27 = 9	8)16 = 2	8)24 = 3
4.	9)18 = 2	4)24 = 6	5)5 = 1	7)28 = 4	1)5 = 5
5.	4)36 = 9	1)9 = 9	7)21 = 3	5)15 = 3	9)36 = 4

Spectrum Division, Grade 4 — Chapter 1, Division Facts through 81 ÷ 9 — 19

Page 20

Division Practice — SCORE /25

Divide.

	a	b	c	d	e
1.	4)36 = 9	6)54 = 9	4)8 = 2	8)16 = 2	2)12 = 6
2.	6)18 = 3	9)81 = 9	4)4 = 1	6)30 = 5	3)9 = 3
3.	7)14 = 2	3)21 = 7	5)40 = 8	3)24 = 8	4)16 = 4
4.	1)5 = 5	3)6 = 2	5)10 = 2	4)12 = 3	5)30 = 6
5.	7)49 = 7	9)63 = 7	4)32 = 8	2)14 = 7	1)8 = 8

Spectrum Division, Grade 4 — Chapter 1, Division Facts through 81 ÷ 9 — 20

Page 21

Division Practice — SCORE /29

Divide.

	a	b	c	d	e
1.	5)20 = 4	1)8 = 8	7)7 = 1	3)27 = 9	5)35 = 7
2.	8)40 = 5	7)21 = 3	9)45 = 5	7)42 = 6	8)64 = 8
3.	2)18 = 9	3)15 = 5	6)12 = 2	6)24 = 4	8)48 = 6
4.	6)6 = 1	2)8 = 4	9)36 = 4	4)20 = 5	2)16 = 8

Find the rule and complete each table.

5.

a — divide by 5

In	Out
30	6
40	8
25	5
45	9
20	4

b — divide by 8

In	Out
8	1
64	8
24	3
56	7
40	5

c — divide by 6

In	Out
36	6
18	3
54	9
42	7
12	2

Spectrum Division, Grade 4 — Chapter 1, Division Facts through 81 ÷ 9 — 21

Page 22

Division Practice — SCORE /25

Divide.

	a	b	c	d	e
1.	1)4 = 4	2)16 = 8	9)63 = 7	7)42 = 6	5)20 = 4
2.	9)54 = 6	9)9 = 1	4)12 = 3	6)6 = 1	9)36 = 4
3.	8)16 = 2	5)25 = 5	2)12 = 6	4)8 = 2	3)6 = 2
4.	8)8 = 1	6)30 = 5	6)18 = 3	6)54 = 9	9)27 = 3
5.	2)14 = 7	2)10 = 5	1)3 = 3	4)20 = 5	3)18 = 6

Spectrum Division, Grade 4 — Chapter 1, Division Facts through 81 ÷ 9 — 22

Answer Key

23

Division Practice

Divide.

	a	b	c	d	e
1.	9 — 8)72	3 — 2)6	8 — 7)56	8 — 3)24	8 — 4)32
2.	9 — 7)63	4 — 4)16	4 — 8)32	6 — 5)30	4 — 2)8
3.	1 — 7)7	3 — 8)24	9 — 3)27	1 — 6)6	8 — 1)8
4.	7 — 5)35	7 — 6)42	6 — 6)36	8 — 8)64	7 — 3)21

Find the rule and complete each table.

5.

a			b			c	
In	Out		In	Out		In	Out
18	2		21	7		7	1
45	5		6	2		42	6
63	7		24	8		35	5
36	4		27	9		56	8
27	3		15	5		49	7

divide by 9   divide by 3   divide by 7

Spectrum Division
Grade 4
Chapter 1
Division Facts through 81 ÷ 9
23

24

💡 **Check What You Learned**

Division Facts through 81 ÷ 9

Divide.

	a	b	c	d	e
1.	6 — 3)18	3 — 9)27	1 — 7)7	8 — 8)64	8 — 5)40
2.	8 — 9)72	6 — 6)36	2 — 8)16	3 — 7)21	7 — 4)28
3.	5 — 5)25	8 — 8)64	6 — 9)54	7 — 5)35	4 — 3)12
4.	7 — 7)49	1 — 9)9	3 — 7)21	9 — 2)18	6 — 3)18
5.	4 — 4)16	5 — 4)20	4 — 9)36	7 — 8)56	6 — 7)42
6.	0 — 9)0	8 — 4)32	9 — 9)81	2 — 5)10	7 — 7)49
7.	4 — 8)32	6 — 9)54	8 — 6)48	8 — 3)24	6 — 4)24
8.	5 — 9)45	9 — 3)27	6 — 5)30	7 — 6)42	2 — 2)4
9.	5 — 8)40	7 — 9)63	7 — 2)14	1 — 3)3	6 — 7)56
10.	6 — 8)48	1 — 7)7	4 — 2)8	9 — 1)9	4 — 7)28

Spectrum Division
Grade 4
Chapter 1
Division Facts through 81 ÷ 9
24

25

🔍 **Check What You Know**

Problem Solving: Division Facts through 81 ÷ 9

Read the problem carefully and solve. Show your work under each question.

Darnell collects stickers. He wants to organize them in a sticker book. He plans to put the same number of stickers on each page. Darnell has 24 sports stickers, 81 animal stickers, 36 fuzzy stickers, and 63 scratch-and-sniff stickers.

1. Darnell can fit 9 animal stickers on a page. How many pages will he use for his animal stickers?

   _____9_____ pages

2. Darnell puts all of his scratch-and-sniff stickers on 7 pages. He puts the same number of stickers on each page. How many stickers are on each page?

   _____9_____ stickers

3. Darnell fits all of his sports stickers onto 3 pages. If each page has the same number of stickers, how many stickers are on each page? What multiplication sentence can Darnell use to check his division?

   _____8_____ stickers

   __3 x 8 = 24__

4. How many pages will Darnell use for his fuzzy stickers if he puts 6 fuzzy stickers on each page?

   _____6_____ pages

Spectrum Division
Grade 4
Chapter 2
Problem Solving: Division Facts through 81 ÷ 9
25

26

Dividing through 45 ÷ 5

Read the problem carefully and solve. Show your work under each question.

Carolyn helps get 4 sailboats ready for a sailing class. She divides the supplies evenly between each sailboat. She has 8 sails and 20 life jackets. All of the sailboats need new ropes for their sails. There are 16 pieces of rope.

Helpful Hint
The division sentence 16 ÷ 2 = 8 can also be written as:

quotient ⟶ 8
divisor ⟶ 2)16 ⟵ dividend

1. Carolyn puts the same number of sails on each boat. How many sails does she put on each sailboat?

   _____2_____ sails

2. The pieces of rope are evenly divided among the boats. How many pieces of rope does each sailboat get?

   _____4_____ pieces of rope

3. Carolyn puts the same number of life jackets on each boat. How many life jackets does she put on each boat?

   _____5_____ life jackets

Spectrum Division
Grade 4
Chapter 2
Problem Solving: Division Facts through 81 ÷ 9
26

27

Dividing through 63 ÷ 7

Read the problem carefully and solve. Show your work under each question.

Michael coaches a tennis program at a summer camp. He divides the campers into 2 teams, beginners and advanced. He has 54 tennis balls to use with the beginner team and 48 balls to use with the advanced team. He always divides the tennis balls evenly between the groups within each team.

1. Michael divides the beginners into 6 groups for a practice drill. How many tennis balls does each group get?

   _____9_____ tennis balls

2. Michael divides the advanced players into 6 groups to practice serving. How many tennis balls does each group get?

   _____8_____ tennis balls

3. The beginners lost 5 tennis balls. Michael divides the players into 7 groups for the next activity. How many tennis balls will each group get?

   _____7_____ tennis balls

Spectrum Division
Grade 4
Chapter 2
Problem Solving: Division Facts through 81 ÷ 9
27

28

Dividing through 81 ÷ 9

Read the problem carefully and solve. Show your work under each question.

Carla fills baskets with flowers for her mom's surprise birthday party. Each of the 8 tables will get a basket. There are 72 pink flowers, 56 yellow flowers, and 64 white flowers. Carla wants to divide the flowers evenly between the baskets.

Helpful Hint
When solving word problems, write an equation to help you find the answer. If you know there are 63 total items to be equally divided between 9 people and you want to know how many items each person gets, you can write the problem like this:

63 ÷ 9 = x
Then, find x by finding the number that makes 63 when multiplied by 9.
9 x 7 = 63   x = 7

1. Carla evenly divides the pink flowers among the baskets. How many pink flowers are in each basket?

   _____9_____ pink flowers

2. Carla notices 16 of the white flowers are too wilted to use. If Carla throws those flowers away, how many white flowers are in each basket? Write a division equation. Then, solve.

   __40 ÷ x = 8__   _____5_____ white flowers

3. After Carla evenly divides the yellow flowers between the baskets, she wants to check to make sure she divided them correctly. What multiplication sentence can Carla use to check her work?

   __7 x 8 = 56__

Spectrum Division
Grade 4
Chapter 2
Problem Solving: Division Facts through 81 ÷ 9
28

Page 29

Division Practice

Read the problem carefully and solve. Show your work under each question.

Appleton School is having a cake and cookie sale. Students are helping to bake the cakes and cookies. They measure and mix the recipes.

1. Delores divides flour into batches to make cakes. She has 18 cups of flour. Each cake takes 2 cups. How many cakes can she make?

   _____9_____ cakes

2. Ella has 21 teaspoons of vanilla. Each batch of cookies takes 3 teaspoons. How many batches of cookies can Ella make from this much vanilla?

   _____7_____ batches

3. Each batch of cookies contains 8 tablespoons of chopped pecans. Marty has 40 tablespoons of chopped pecans. How many batches of cookies can she make with the pecans?

   _____5_____ batches

Spectrum Division
Grade 4
Chapter 2
Problem Solving: Division Facts through 81 ÷ 9
29

Page 30

Division Practice

Solve each problem. Show your work under each question.

1. Mrs. Blair is planning a yard party. Her big punch bowl holds 40 glasses of punch. If she wants to allow 5 glasses for each guest, how many guests will the punch bowl serve?

   The punch bowl will serve _____8_____ guests.

2. At the rodeo, 32 people signed up for bronco riding. The 4 horses will give the same number of rides. How many rides will each horse give? Write a division equation. Then, solve.

   _____32 ÷ x = 4_____

   Each horse will give _____8_____ rides.

3. Mr. Ferris is packing to move to a new house. He has 35 pairs of shoes. He can pack 7 pairs of shoes in a box. How many boxes will he need for his shoes?

   Mr. Ferris will need _____5_____ boxes for his shoes.

Spectrum Division
Grade 4
30
Chapter 2
Problem Solving: Division Facts through 81 ÷ 9

Page 31

Division Practice

Solve each problem. Show your work under each question.

1. At the local fair, 72 people waited in line for a boat ride. The boat can hold 8 people. How many trips will the boat have to take for everyone to get a ride?

   The boat will have to take _____9_____ trips.

2. The Davis brothers found 27 cars when they cleaned out their toy closet. They want to give the same number of cars to each of their 3 cousins. How many cars will each cousin get?

   Each cousin will get _____9_____ toy cars.

3. Mrs. Gomez sold 18 pet lizards this week at her pet store. If 9 customers bought the same number of lizards, how many lizards did each person take home? Write a division equation. Then, solve.

   _____18 ÷ x = 9_____

   Each person took home _____2_____ lizards.

Spectrum Division
Grade 4
Chapter 2
Problem Solving: Division Facts through 81 ÷ 9
31

Page 32

Division Practice

Solve each problem. Show your work under each question.

1. Eddie and Toru listened to 72 of their favorite songs. If there were 9 songs on each CD, how many CDs did they listen to?

   They listened to _____8_____ CDs.

2. Mr. Luiz printed 35 tests for his students. If there were 7 rows of students, how many tests were passed out to each row?

   There were _____5_____ tests passed out to each row.

3. Gary opened a bag of candy containing 81 pieces. He wants to give each of his guests the same number of pieces. If he has 9 guests, how many pieces does each person get?

   Each guest gets _____9_____ pieces.

Spectrum Division
Grade 4
32
Chapter 2
Problem Solving: Division Facts through 81 ÷ 9

Page 33

Division Practice

Solve each problem. Show your work under each question.

1. Last year, Mrs. Ford decided to give chores to each person in the family. Each person got the same number of chores. There are 8 family members. If there were 32 chores, how many did each person get?

   Each person got _____4_____ chores.

2. It takes 16 hours to drive to the dunes. Tasha and her brother Kurt will drive the same number of hours. How many hours will each of them drive?

   Each of them will drive _____8_____ hours.

3. The Pet Store warehouse received 63 boxes of cat litter. The same number of boxes will be sent to 9 stores. How many boxes will each store get? Write a division equation. Then, solve.

   _____63 ÷ x = 9_____

   Each store will get _____7_____ boxes.

Spectrum Division
Grade 4
Chapter 2
Problem Solving: Division Facts through 81 ÷ 9
33

Page 34

Division Practice

Solve each problem. Show your work under each question.

1. Lori found 42 shells at the beach. She gave the same number of shells to 7 of her friends. How many shells did she give to each friend?

   She gave _____6_____ shells to each friend.

2. The drama club is giving a party in the school lunchroom. The club wants to be seated in groups of 8. If 64 students go to the party, how many groups of students will there be?

   The drama club will have _____8_____ groups of students.

3. The Pancake Restaurant served 32 pancakes. If 8 customers ate an equal number of pancakes, how many did each person eat?

   Each person ate _____4_____ pancakes.

Spectrum Division
Grade 4
Chapter 2
Problem Solving: Division Facts through 81 ÷ 9

Answer Key

Page 35

NAME _____

SCORE ● / 3

Division Practice

Solve each problem. Show your work under each question.

1. In the flower seed package, there are 48 seeds. Alicia has 8 flowerpots. She wants to put an equal number of seeds in each pot. How many seeds should she put in each pot?

She should put _____6_____ seeds in each pot.

2. The local baseball team has a supply of 54 baseballs for 9 home games. How many baseballs are available for each home game?

There are _____6_____ baseballs available for each home game.

3. The class gerbil has just had 16 babies. If there are 8 students who want to take them home, how many babies can each student have?

Each student can have _____2_____ baby gerbils.

Spectrum Division
Grade 4

Chapter 2
Problem Solving: Division Facts through 81 ÷ 9
35

35

Page 36

NAME _____

Check What You Learned

Problem Solving: Division Facts through 81 ÷ 9

Read the problem carefully and solve. Show your work under each question.

The marching bands from four area schools are in a large parade. Each band marches in rows with the same number of students in each row. Leo's school band has 45 members. Taro's school band has 72 members. Maya's school band has 32 members, and Barbara's school band has 63 members.

1. Maya's school band marches in 4 rows. How many band members are there in each row?

_____8_____ band members

2. Taro's school band marches with 9 band members in each row. How many rows does the band have? Write a division equation. Then, solve.

$72 ÷ x = 9$

_____8_____ rows

3. Barbara's band director plans to have 7 rows. How many band members are in each row? What multiplication sentence can be used to check this division?

_____9_____ band members

$7 × 9 = 63$

4. Leo's school band also marches with 9 band members in each row. How many rows does the band have?

_____5_____ rows

Spectrum Division
Grade 4

Chapter 2
Problem Solving: Division Facts through 81 ÷ 9
36

36

Page 37

NAME _____

Mid-Test Chapters 1–2

Divide.

	a	b	c	d	e
1.	5)25 → 5	4)16 → 4	7)21 → 3	9)81 → 9	3)18 → 3
2.	6)54 → 9	3)27 → 9	9)72 → 8	7)49 → 7	5)5 → 5
3.	3)24 → 8	4)28 → 4	9)36 → 4	2)14 → 2	1)9 → 9
4.	3)6 → 2	8)16 → 2	7)35 → 5	5)15 → 3	3)9 → 3
5.	7)42 → 6	9)45 → 5	2)2 → 1	7)63 → 9	2)6 → 3
6.	5)20 → 4	2)18 → 9	8)32 → 4	4)24 → 6	8)72 → 9
7.	1)1 → 1	8)64 → 8	6)36 → 6	5)45 → 9	2)16 → 8
8.	8)48 → 6	3)15 → 5	3)21 → 7	9)54 → 6	1)5 → 5
9.	8)24 → 3	7)28 → 4	4)36 → 9	7)14 → 2	9)9 → 1
10.	5)35 → 7	6)42 → 7	5)45 → 9	1)2 → 2	9)63 → 7

Spectrum Division
Grade 4

Mid-Test
Chapters 1–2
37

37

Page 38

NAME _____

Mid-Test Chapters 1–2

Solve each problem. Show your work under each question.

11. A group of 7 boys cut lawns over the weekend. They made 56 dollars. Each boy will make the same amount. How much money will each boy get?

Each boy will get _____8_____ dollars.

12. Gloria decided to make lemonade for her family. There are 8 people in her family. The pitcher will hold 24 glasses of lemonade. How many glasses can each person have? Write a division equation. Then, solve.

$24 ÷ x = 8$

Each person can have _____3_____ glasses.

13. Susan, Marta, and Aisha have 5 hours to spend at the zoo. There are 40 different animals they want to see. During each hour at the zoo, how many animals should they plan to see?

They should plan to see _____8_____ different animals each hour.

14. Write the rule for this table.

In	Out
48	8
24	4
42	7
18	3

divide by 6

Spectrum Division
Grade 4

Mid-Test
Chapters 1–2
38

38

Page 39

NAME _____

Check What You Know

Dividing through 4 Digits by 1 Digit

Divide.

	a	b	c	d	e
1.	2)42 → 21	2)15 → 7r1	2)142 → 71	3)63 → 21	3)180 → 60
2.	5)152 → 30r2	3)521 → 173r2	8)55 → 6r7	7)70 → 10	4)98 → 24r2
3.	9)87 → 9r6	7)77 → 11	2)50 → 25	2)8142 → 4087	3)900 → 300
4.	3)45 → 15	5)105 → 21	5)6500 → 1300	8)78 → 9r6	3)68 → 22r2
5.	5)1905 → 381	6)121 → 20r1	7)62 → 8r6	7)22 → 3r1	2)90 → 45

Spectrum Division
Grade 4

Chapter 3
Dividing through 4 Digits by 1 Digit
39

39

Page 40

NAME _____

SCORE ● / 20

Dividing 2 Digits

x	1	2	3	4	5
8	8	16	24	32	40

```
        4                             4 r 1
8)33    33 is between 32    Since 33 − 32 = 1    8)33
  −32   and 40, so 33 ÷ 8   and 1 is less than 8, the   −32
8 × 4   is between 4 and 5.  remainder 1 is recorded       1
Subtract. The ones digit is 4.   like this.
```

Divide.

	a	b	c	d	e
1.	5)26 → 5r1	7)58 → 8r2	4)31 → 7r3	9)82 → 9r1	6)35 → 5r5
2.	8)66 → 8r2	3)17 → 5r2	2)13 → 6r1	7)50 → 7r1	6)40 → 6r4
3.	9)30 → 3r3	5)41 → 8r1	3)10 → 3r1	8)73 → 9r1	7)57 → 8r1
4.	8)20 → 2r4	6)37 → 6r1	9)55 → 6r1	7)29 → 4r1	5)47 → 9r2

Spectrum Division
Grade 4

Chapter 3
Dividing through 4 Digits by 1 Digit
40

40

Spectrum Division
Grade 4

Answer Key

89

Answer Key

41

Dividing 2 Digits

Divide.

	a	b	c	d	e
1.	18 / 2)36	15r1 / 5)76	11r2 / 7)79	24 / 4)96	13r2 / 7)93
2.	17r1 / 5)86	32 / 3)96	12r3 / 8)99	12 / 7)84	25 / 3)75
3.	15r3 / 6)93	12 / 6)72	11r1 / 8)89	12r5 / 7)89	11 / 9)99
4.	22 / 4)88	28 / 3)84	38r1 / 2)77	19r2 / 4)78	11r5 / 8)93

Spectrum Division
Grade 4
Chapter 3
Dividing through 4 Digits by 1 Digit
41

42

Division Practice

Divide.

	a	b	c	d	e
1.	4r1 / 4)17	7r1 / 3)22	5r1 / 4)21	9r2 / 3)29	6r2 / 4)26
2.	4r2 / 8)34	3r3 / 8)27	7r2 / 4)30	3r2 / 7)23	6r2 / 5)32
3.	8r2 / 3)26	7r3 / 5)38	6r2 / 3)20	9r1 / 4)37	4r2 / 9)38
4.	3r3 / 6)21	8r2 / 5)42	5r1 / 5)26	8r3 / 4)35	7r1 / 2)15
5.	4r1 / 7)29	5r3 / 9)48	4r2 / 5)22	3r1 / 9)28	5r4 / 6)34

Spectrum Division
Grade 4
Chapter 3
Dividing through 4 Digits by 1 Digit
42

43

Division Practice

Divide.

	a	b	c	d	e
1.	4r2 / 7)30	5r3 / 8)43	8r3 / 9)75	4r2 / 6)26	5r2 / 5)27
2.	3r2 / 8)26	8r4 / 6)52	4r3 / 9)39	8r2 / 4)34	5r3 / 9)48
3.	5r3 / 7)38	7r1 / 3)22	7r2 / 5)37	6r2 / 6)38	5r3 / 6)33
4.	8r2 / 3)26	7r2 / 8)58	7r2 / 7)51	9r3 / 9)84	7r2 / 4)30
5.	5r2 / 4)22	7r1 / 9)64	7r3 / 6)45	8r2 / 8)66	9r2 / 7)65

Spectrum Division
Grade 4
Chapter 3
Dividing through 4 Digits by 1 Digit
43

44

Division Practice

Divide.

	a	b	c	d	e
1.	9r2 / 8)74	6r2 / 5)32	8r2 / 6)50	6r2 / 3)20	5r5 / 9)50
2.	8r3 / 7)59	9r2 / 4)38	6r2 / 8)50	6r3 / 4)27	5r2 / 9)47
3.	7r5 / 8)61	5r5 / 7)40	9r3 / 6)57	9r1 / 9)82	5r1 / 2)11
4.	6r6 / 7)48	8r1 / 9)73	9r2 / 5)47	7r2 / 6)44	9r5 / 7)68
5.	5r2 / 3)17	5r7 / 7)47	5r1 / 6)31	8r3 / 5)43	9r6 / 9)87

Spectrum Division
Grade 4
Chapter 3
Dividing through 4 Digits by 1 Digit
44

45

Division Practice

Divide.

	a	b	c	d	e
1.	22r2 / 3)68	28r2 / 3)86	23r1 / 2)47	11r2 / 5)57	11r1 / 8)89
2.	31r2 / 3)95	11r2 / 7)79	32r1 / 2)65	21r3 / 4)87	12r1 / 3)37
3.	11r4 / 5)59	43r1 / 2)87	11r1 / 4)45	21r1 / 3)64	41r1 / 2)83
4.	12r1 / 8)97	13r1 / 6)79	16r1 / 4)65	13r4 / 7)95	24r2 / 3)74
5.	14r2 / 5)72	26r1 / 2)53	12r2 / 7)86	15r2 / 3)47	13r3 / 6)81

Spectrum Division
Grade 4
Chapter 3
Dividing through 4 Digits by 1 Digit
45

46

Division Practice

Divide.

	a	b	c	d	e
1.	15r2 / 6)92	15r3 / 4)63	18r1 / 2)37	13r5 / 7)96	18r2 / 3)56
2.	12r3 / 5)63	12r3 / 8)99	13r3 / 4)55	14r1 / 6)85	14r4 / 5)74
3.	37r1 / 2)75	23r3 / 4)95	11r5 / 7)82	28r1 / 3)85	11r7 / 9)95
4.	18r3 / 4)75	16r2 / 5)82	25r2 / 3)77	14r5 / 6)89	28r1 / 2)57
5.	13r2 / 7)93	14r4 / 5)74	46r1 / 2)93	16r3 / 4)67	14r1 / 3)43

Spectrum Division
Grade 4
Chapter 3
Dividing through 4 Digits by 1 Digit
46

Answer Key

NAME

Page 47 — SCORE / 25

Division Practice
Divide.

	a	b	c	d	e
1.	3r1 2)63	15 5)75	10r7 9)97	12r4 7)88	11r1 5)56
2.	24 3)72	12 8)96	13 6)78	16r1 4)65	19r2 5)97
3.	37r1 2)75	8r2 4)34	15r3 6)93	11r1 8)89	34r1 2)69
4.	21r1 3)64	12r3 7)87	19 5)95	11r3 4)47	19r2 3)59
5.	14r3 4)59	11r5 6)71	24r1 2)49	14r1 7)99	12r1 8)97

Spectrum Division
Grade 4
Chapter 3
Dividing through 4 Digits by 1 Digit
47

Page 48 — SCORE / 15

Dividing 3 Digits
Divide.

Since 100 × 8 = 800 and 800 is greater than 453, there is no hundreds digit.

8)453

x	10	20	30	40	50	60
8	80	160	240	320	400	480

453 is between 400 and 480. 453 ÷ 8 is between 50 and 60. The tens digit is 5.

x	1	2	3	4	5	6	7
8	8	16	24	32	40	48	56

53 is between 48 and 56. 53 ÷ 8 is between 6 and 7. The ones digit is 6.

```
      5
8)453
  -40    8 × 5 = 40
   53  Subtract
```

```
     56 r5
8)453
  -40    8 × 6 = 48
   53  Subtract
  -48
    5  Remainder
```

Divide.

	a	b	c	d	e
1.	90 8)720	93 4)372	41r3 9)372	43r1 4)173	75 2)150
2.	92 6)552	46r1 3)139	62 4)248	98r8 9)890	21 5)105
3.	86r6 9)780	45 5)225	90r3 9)813	73 7)511	36r2 3)110

Spectrum Division
Grade 4
48
Chapter 3
Dividing through 4 Digits by 1 Digit

Page 49 — SCORE / 20

Dividing 3 Digits
Divide.

	a	b	c	d	e
1.	109r1 5)546	190r2 4)762	157r1 3)472	114r3 6)687	124r2 8)994
2.	311 3)933	114 4)456	115r1 7)806	225r1 2)451	150 5)750
3.	104 9)936	256 3)768	101r6 9)915	212 4)848	127 6)762
4.	417r1 2)835	176 2)352	109r3 7)766	126r2 4)506	143r1 2)287

Spectrum Division
Grade 4
Chapter 3
Dividing through 4 Digits by 1 Digit
49

Page 50 — SCORE / 25

Division Practice
Divide.

	a	b	c	d	e
1.	128r5 6)773	449 2)898	141r2 4)566	130r1 6)781	324 3)972
2.	158r1 2)317	183 4)732	109r8 9)989	128r1 7)897	197 2)394
3.	105r4 5)529	112r1 8)897	225r1 3)676	174 2)348	155 6)930
4.	261r1 3)784	157r3 5)788	160r1 3)481	111r3 5)558	305 2)610
5.	108 3)324	190r3 5)953	144r4 6)868	325 3)975	120 6)720

Spectrum Division
Grade 4
50
Chapter 3
Dividing through 4 Digits by 1 Digit

Page 51 — SCORE / 25

Division Practice
Divide.

	a	b	c	d	e
1.	75 3)225	54 6)324	32 9)288	69 2)138	65 7)455
2.	54 4)216	63 8)504	54 5)270	57 3)171	63 6)378
3.	95 9)855	97 2)194	55 7)385	76 4)304	87 5)435
4.	67 3)201	58 6)348	93 8)744	77 2)154	34 9)306
5.	56 4)224	92 7)644	95 5)475	94 3)282	98 6)588

Spectrum Division
Grade 4
Chapter 3
Dividing through 4 Digits by 1 Digit
51

Page 52 — SCORE / 25

Division Practice
Divide.

	a	b	c	d	e
1.	77r1 2)155	89r2 4)358	45r3 6)273	53r4 8)428	44r3 9)399
2.	98r2 3)296	58r1 5)291	78r3 7)549	86r1 2)173	87r4 5)439
3.	84r2 9)758	65r2 6)392	39r6 7)279	69r2 3)209	57r3 4)231
4.	87r3 8)699	59r1 2)119	84r3 6)507	39r2 5)197	54r3 9)489
5.	57r2 3)173	58r2 7)408	39r3 6)237	67r3 5)338	78r2 4)314

Spectrum Division
Grade 4
52
Chapter 3
Dividing through 4 Digits by 1 Digit

Spectrum Division
Grade 4

Answer Key

Answer Key

Page 53

Division Practice — SCORE / 25

Divide.

	a	b	c	d	e
1.	66r4 8)532	67r1 4)269	93r4 6)562	89r1 2)179	73r2 9)659
2.	39r2 3)119	62r5 7)439	96r4 5)484	38r3 4)155	65r2 9)587
3.	94r5 8)757	78r1 2)157	47r2 3)143	56r2 6)338	96r1 2)193
4.	47r2 7)331	32r3 9)291	25r2 8)202	95r3 4)383	74r2 3)224
5.	74r4 5)374	89r3 6)537	96r3 9)867	67r1 2)135	74r2 6)446

Spectrum Division / Grade 4 / 53 — Chapter 3 / Dividing through 4 Digits by 1 Digit

Page 54

Division Practice — SCORE / 25

Divide.

	a	b	c	d	e
1.	216 2)432	231 4)924	121 6)726	115 5)575	152 3)456
2.	112 7)784	111 9)999	112 8)896	212 4)848	476 2)952
3.	143 5)715	314 3)942	131 6)786	153 5)765	233 4)932
4.	253 3)759	363 2)726	117 5)585	112 7)784	274 2)548
5.	162 6)972	242 4)968	373 2)746	112 8)896	214 4)856

Spectrum Division / Grade 4 / 54 — Chapter 3 / Dividing through 4 Digits by 1 Digit

Page 55

Division Practice — SCORE / 25

Divide.

	a	b	c	d	e
1.	218r1 2)437	123r1 6)739	244r3 4)979	198r4 5)994	198r2 3)596
2.	112r3 8)899	114r6 7)804	146r3 6)879	146r4 5)734	376r1 2)753
3.	148r3 4)595	249r1 3)748	139r5 7)978	147r5 6)887	189r3 4)759
4.	268r1 2)537	137r2 5)687	112r1 8)897	158r3 4)635	278r2 3)836
5.	114r5 6)689	189r1 2)379	149r3 5)748	113r3 8)907	164r3 6)987

Spectrum Division / Grade 4 / 55 — Chapter 3 / Dividing through 4 Digits by 1 Digit

Page 56

Division Practice — SCORE / 25

Divide.

	a	b	c	d	e
1.	248r2 3)746	113r5 7)796	178r3 5)893	235r3 4)943	112r4 6)676
2.	122r2 8)978	168r1 2)337	136r5 7)957	148r2 3)446	134r2 4)538
3.	126r3 6)759	136r4 5)684	111r6 8)894	243r1 2)487	317r2 3)953
4.	157r3 6)945	157r1 4)629	125r4 7)879	189r2 5)947	475r1 2)951
5.	184r3 4)739	215r2 3)647	142r5 6)857	429r1 2)859	234r2 4)938

Spectrum Division / Grade 4 / 56 — Chapter 3 / Dividing through 4 Digits by 1 Digit

Page 57

Division Practice — SCORE / 25

Divide.

	a	b	c	d	e
1.	10r5 6)65	10r4 9)94	308r1 3)925	80r4 7)564	205r3 4)823
2.	50r3 5)253	108r1 8)865	420r1 2)841	10r5 7)75	60r4 6)364
3.	103r2 4)414	50r4 5)254	40r7 8)327	207r2 3)623	230r1 2)461
4.	60r3 7)423	104r3 6)627	105r4 5)529	210r2 4)842	320r1 3)961
5.	40r5 8)325	105r3 7)738	70r3 6)423	120r1 2)241	107r4 5)539

Spectrum Division / Grade 4 / 57 — Chapter 3 / Dividing through 4 Digits by 1 Digit

Page 58

Dividing 4 Digits — SCORE / 12

$8 \div 4 = 2$ $9 \div 4 = 2$ remainder 1 $11 \div 4 = 2$ remainder 3 $37 \div 4 = 9$ remainder 1
$4 \times 2 = 8$

(worked example: 2229 ← quotient, divisor / dividend, 4)8917, 1 ← remainder)

Divide.

	a	b	c	d
1.	1550 3)4650	654r1 6)3925	185r7 8)1487	4617 2)9234
2.	928 7)6496	2142 4)8568	203r5 7)1426	1248r2 3)3746
3.	1700r3 5)8503	699r1 9)6292	791r2 4)3166	1158r1 2)2317

Spectrum Division / Grade 4 / 58 — Chapter 3 / Dividing through 4 Digits by 1 Digit

Answer Key

Page 59 — Division Practice

Divide.

	a	b	c	d
1.	2)3486 = 1743	4)8572 = 2143	6)3764 = 627r2	5)5328 = 1065r3
2.	3)2874 = 958	2)8497 = 4248r1	7)8598 = 1228r2	2)8040 = 4020
3.	4)2988 = 747	6)8149 = 1358r1	7)5001 = 714r3	3)6238 = 2079r1
4.	5)7384 = 1476r4	8)4376 = 547	2)4811 = 2405r1	4)1583 = 395r3
5.	6)7391 = 1231r5	3)6943 = 2314r1	7)4795 = 685	5)5237 = 1047r2

Spectrum Division Grade 4 — Chapter 3, Dividing through 4 Digits by 1 Digit 59

59

Page 60 — Division Practice (SCORE / 20)

Divide.

	a	b	c	d
1.	8)3216 = 402	4)1272 = 318	7)1502 = 214r4	3)296 = 98r2
2.	6)4811 = 801r5	9)788 = 87r5	5)554 = 110r4	8)1143 = 142r7
3.	4)362 = 90r2	3)1553 = 517r2	6)5554 = 925r4	7)487 = 69r4
4.	2)1694 = 847	4)1550 = 387r2	9)7155 = 795	5)2093 = 418r3
5.	7)4778 = 682r4	3)316 = 105r1	6)483 = 80r3	4)515 = 128r3

Spectrum Division Grade 4 — Chapter 3, Dividing through 4 Digits by 1 Digit 60

60

Page 61 — Division Practice (SCORE / 20)

Divide.

	a	b	c	d
1.	5)2013 = 402r3	8)1886 = 235r6	9)2591 = 287r8	7)3330 = 475r5
2.	2)219 = 109r1	3)632 = 210r2	5)1835 = 367	8)567 = 70r7
3.	6)6150 = 1025	4)1278 = 319r2	5)4250 = 850	2)819 = 409r1
4.	9)1123 = 124r7	7)2273 = 324r5	8)1126 = 140r6	3)8693 = 2897r2
5.	4)2086 = 521r2	6)2464 = 410r4	9)1088 = 120r8	8)9198 = 1149r6

Spectrum Division Grade 4 — Chapter 3, Dividing through 4 Digits by 1 Digit 61

61

Page 62 — Division and Place Value (SCORE / 24)

Use patterns of place value to help determine the divisor.

If, 8 ÷ __2__ = 4

Then, using place value, you can find the divisor in greater numbers.

80 ÷ __2__ = 40 ⟶ 80 ÷ 2 = 40
800 ÷ __2__ = 400 ⟶ 800 ÷ 2 = 400
8000 ÷ __2__ = 4000 ⟶ 8000 ÷ 2 = 4000

Fill in the missing numbers.

	a	b
1.	7 ÷ __7__ = 1	6 ÷ __3__ = 2
	70 ÷ __7__ = 10	60 ÷ __3__ = 20
	700 ÷ __7__ = 100	600 ÷ __3__ = 200
	7000 ÷ __7__ = 1000	6000 ÷ __3__ = 2000
2.	12 ÷ __4__ = 3	10 ÷ __5__ = 2
	120 ÷ __4__ = 30	100 ÷ __5__ = 20
	1200 ÷ __4__ = 300	1000 ÷ __5__ = 200
	12000 ÷ __4__ = 3000	10000 ÷ __5__ = 2000
3.	9 ÷ __3__ = 3	5 ÷ __5__ = 1
	90 ÷ __3__ = 30	50 ÷ __5__ = 10
	900 ÷ __3__ = 300	500 ÷ __5__ = 100
	9000 ÷ __3__ = 3000	5000 ÷ __5__ = 1000

Spectrum Division Grade 4 — Chapter 3, Dividing through 4 Digits by 1 Digit 62

62

Page 63 — Division and Place Value (SCORE / 20)

Divide.

	a	b	c	d
1.	3)300 = 100	2)6000 = 3000	2)20 = 10	4)800 = 200
2.	10)400 = 40	300)9000 = 30	40)1200 = 30	10)100 = 10
3.	7)140 = 20	2)80 = 40	700)1400 = 2	40)120 = 3
4.	3)900 = 300	600)1800 = 3	2000)10000 = 5	30)600 = 20
5.	8)1600 = 200	20)140 = 7	90)180 = 2	30)90 = 3

Spectrum Division Grade 4 — Chapter 3, Dividing through 4 Digits by 1 Digit 63

63

Page 64 — Division Practice (SCORE / 20)

Divide.

	a	b	c	d
1.	3)45 = 15	9)72 = 8	2)34 = 16r2	4)76 = 18r4
2.	6)493 = 82r1	3)873 = 291	7)875 = 125	5)987 = 197r2
3.	7)2598 = 371r1	2)5282 = 2641	6)5631 = 938r3	4)9637 = 2409r1
4.	6)9832 = 1638r4	8)5000 = 625	5)7004 = 1400r4	7)5111 = 730r1
5.	5)85 = 17	8)800 = 100	5)2515 = 503	8)9840 = 1230

Spectrum Division Grade 4 — Chapter 3, Dividing through 4 Digits by 1 Digit 64

64

Page 65

NAME _____ SCORE ⬤ / 16

Estimating Quotients

$7\overline{)24}$ Think of what you can round the dividend (24) to so that it is easy to mentally divide by the divisor (7). The quotient is 3.

$7\overline{)21}$
$\underline{-21}$
0
3

$5\overline{)378}$ Think of what you can round the dividend (378) to so that it is easy to mentally divide by the divisor (5).

quotient → 7.6
$5\overline{)380}$
$\underline{-35}$
30
$\underline{-30}$
0

Divide.

	a	b	c	d
1.	5, $3\overline{)116}$	5, $7\overline{)36}$	25, $3\overline{)74}$	21, $4\overline{)83}$
2.	7, $4\overline{)27}$	40, $6\overline{)217}$	60, $8\overline{)481}$	110, $7\overline{)764}$
3.	40, $9\overline{)362}$	280, $2\overline{)563}$	300, $4\overline{)1378}$	1400, $3\overline{)4269}$
4.	300, $8\overline{)2448}$	1800, $5\overline{)9216}$	400, $9\overline{)3502}$	1500, $5\overline{)7358}$

Spectrum Division
Grade 4
Chapter 3
Dividing through 4 Digits by 1 Digit
65

65

Page 66

NAME _____

🔍 **Check What You Learned**

Dividing through 4 Digits by 1 Digit

Divide.

	a	b	c	d	e
1.	16, $2\overline{)32}$	3000, $3\overline{)9000}$	16r1, $3\overline{)49}$	12r1, $8\overline{)97}$	89, $2\overline{)178}$
2.	1530r1, $4\overline{)6121}$	133, $6\overline{)798}$	111r2, $5\overline{)557}$	106, $6\overline{)636}$	111r1, $8\overline{)889}$
3.	48, $2\overline{)96}$	29, $3\overline{)87}$	200, $8\overline{)1600}$	14, $3\overline{)42}$	4r3, $7\overline{)31}$
4.	9r3, $8\overline{)75}$	9r1, $2\overline{)19}$	5r3, $8\overline{)43}$	9r8, $9\overline{)89}$	20, $3\overline{)60}$
5.	201, $3\overline{)603}$	20, $5\overline{)100}$	127, $6\overline{)762}$	5r2, $7\overline{)37}$	24, $2\overline{)48}$

CHAPTER 3 POSTTEST

Spectrum Division
Grade 4
Chapter 3
Dividing through 4 Digits by 1 Digit
66

66

Page 67

NAME _____

🔍 **Check What You Know**

Problem Solving: Dividing through 4 Digits by 1 Digit

Read the problem carefully and solve. Show your work under each question.

A bookstore needs to pack books in boxes to ship. Each box can only hold one type of book. Each type of book must be divided evenly between the boxes. There are 167 nonfiction books and 89 mystery books. There are 35 picture books and 108 fiction books.

1. If the mystery books are packed in 6 boxes, how many mystery books will be in each box? How many mystery books will be left over?

    14 mystery books

    5 books left over

2. If 8 picture books can fit into each box, how many boxes can they fill? How many total boxes will the store need to ship all of the picture books? Explain your answer.

    4 full boxes

    5 total number of boxes needed

    The bookstore will need 1 extra box to ship the remaining 3 books.

3. The bookstore plans to use 7 boxes to ship the nonfiction books. How many nonfiction books will fit in each box? How many will be left over?

    23 nonfiction books

    6 books left over

4. The store only has 3 boxes left to ship all the fiction books. Will all the fiction books fit or will there be some left over? Explain your answer.

    Yes, all boxes will fit. There will be 36 books in each box with no boxes left over.

CHAPTER 4 PRETEST

Spectrum Division
Grade 4
Chapter 4
Problem Solving: Dividing through 4 Digits by 1 Digit
67

67

Page 68

NAME _____ SCORE ⬤ / 5

Dividing 2 Digits

Read the problem carefully and solve. Show your work under each question.

Two different soccer teams need to carpool to the next game. There are 16 players on Molly's team. Each car on Molly's team can hold 5 players. There are 18 players on Lian's team. Each car on Lian's team can hold 4 players. Lian's team has 4 cars.

Helpful Hint
If a number does not divide into another number evenly, there will be a remainder (r).

$7\overline{)22}$
$\underline{-21}$
1
$3\text{ r }1$

1. How many cars can Molly's team fill? How many players will be left over?

    3 full cars

    1 player left

2. How many cars will Molly's team need to take all the players to the game? Explain your answer.

    4 cars

    Her team will need 1 extra car to bring the remaining player.

3. Does Lian's team have enough cars to take all their players to the game? If not, how many players still need a ride?

    No, her team does not have enough cars. Two players will still need a ride.

Spectrum Division
Grade 4
Chapter 4
68

68

Page 69

NAME _____ SCORE ⬤ / 4

Dividing 3 Digits

Read the problem carefully and solve. Show your work under each question.

Natalia and Manuel have a large stamp collection. They organize their stamps into one album. They put the same number of each type of stamp on a page. Natalia and Manuel have 274 animal stamps, 108 sports stamps, 148 flower stamps, and 324 stamps of famous people and events.

Helpful Hint
Remember to write the first digit of the quotient in the correct spot.

$7\overline{)434}$
62

Since $100 \times 7 = 700$ and 700 is greater than 437, there is no hundreds digit in the quotient.

1. Natalia wants to use 8 pages of the album for the animal stamps. How many animal stamps will be on each page? How many animal stamps will be left over?

    34 stamps on a page

    2 stamps left over

2. Manuel decides to use 4 pages of the album for sports stamps. How many sports stamps will be on each page? How many sports stamps will be left over?

    27 stamps on a page

    0 stamps left over

Spectrum Division
Grade 4
Chapter 4
Problem Solving: Dividing through 4 Digits by 1 Digit
69

69

Page 70

NAME _____ SCORE ⬤ / 3

Dividing 4 Digits

Read the problem carefully and solve. Show your work under each question.

Middle City Hardware is having a big sale. The staff workers are putting tools and other items in groups for the sale.

1. Josie's boss gives her 3,258 bolts. Her boss says to put the bolts in bags of 9 bolts each. How many full bags of bolts will she have?

    362 bags

2. Chad has 1,137 screwdrivers. Chad puts them in sets of 4. How many screwdrivers will be left over when he is finished?

    1 left over

3. Special sale items are worth $7,527 in all. The sale will last for 3 days. How much money will the store make per day if the sales are equal each day?

    $2509

Spectrum Division
Grade 4
Chapter 4
Problem Solving: Dividing through 4 Digits by 1 Digit
70

70

Answer Key

NAME
SCORE ⬤ / 3

Division and Place Value

Solve each problem. Show your work under each question.

1. The cross-country team runs 70 miles a week. If they stop for a break every 7 miles, how many breaks do they take each week?

   They take ___10___ breaks each week.

2. The pool's lap lane is 800 feet long. If a swimmer splits this length into 4 equal sections, how many feet will each section be?

   Each section will be ___200___ feet.

3. The garden show is moving into a bigger area. The new area has 1,200 square feet of space for displays. There are 300 different displays, and each display will need the same amount of space. How many square feet does each display get?

   Each display gets ___4___ square feet of space.

Spectrum Division
Grade 4
Problem Solving: Dividing through 4 Digits by 1 Digit
71

71

NAME
SCORE ⬤ / 4

Division Practice

Solve each problem. Show your work under each question.

1. A boys' club picked up litter in the park. They collected 913 bags of litter. If each boy collected about the same amount, about how many bags did the 7 boys collect? How many extra bags were collected?

   Each boy picked up about ___130___ bags.

   There were ___3___ extra bags collected.

2. The school supply store received a shipment of 730 pens. If the pens are packed in 5 boxes, how many pens are in each box?

   There are ___146___ pens in each box.

3. Taylor needs 612 more dollars to buy a plane ticket to visit his cousin in Australia. If he saves 9 dollars a day, how soon can he go to Australia?

   He will have the rest of the money in ___68___ days.

Spectrum Division
Grade 4
Problem Solving: Dividing through 4 Digits by 1 Digit
72

72

NAME
SCORE ⬤ / 4

Division Practice

Solve each problem. Show your work under each question.

1. The school office received 22 computers. If there are 9 classrooms receiving the computers, how many computers will go to each classroom? How many computers will be left?

   Each classroom will receive ___2___ computers.

   There will be ___4___ extra computers.

2. There are 60 summer jobs for lifeguards at the city pools. There will be 3 lifeguards at each city pool. How many city pools are there?

   There are ___20___ city pools.

3. At the Hot Dog Shack, customers bought 27 hot dogs on Saturday. There were only 9 customers. How many hot dogs did each customer buy?

   Each customer bought ___3___ hot dogs.

Spectrum Division
Grade 4
Problem Solving: Dividing through 4 Digits by 1 Digit
73

73

NAME
SCORE ⬤ / 4

Division Practice

Solve each problem. Show your work under each question.

1. The school spirit club baked cakes for a charity event. There were 75 different types of cakes. Each baker baked the same number of cakes. If there were 5 bakers, how many cakes did each baker make?

   Each baker made ___15___ cakes.

2. The Fish Shop is open 72 hours a week. The shop is open 6 days a week and the same number of hours each day. How many hours each day is the shop open?

   The shop is open ___12___ hours a day.

3. The glee club needs to sell 382 tickets to win a trip. If there are 8 members who want to go on the trip, how many tickets does each member need to sell? How many extra tickets will be left?

   Each member needs to sell ___47___ tickets.

   There will be ___6___ extra tickets.

Spectrum Division
Grade 4
Problem Solving: Dividing through 4 Digits by 1 Digit
74

74

NAME
SCORE ⬤ / 3

Estimating Quotients

Read the problem carefully and solve. Show your work under each question.

The Quick Haul Trucking Company makes local deliveries. The shipping manager divides all of the boxes into various shipments. Sometimes, the manager makes estimates for the shipments.

> **Helpful Hint**
>
> To estimate a quotient, round the dividend into a number that is easily divided by the divisor.
> To estimate the quotient of 45 divided by 7, first round 45 into 42. Then, a good estimate of the quotient is 6.

1. Quick Haul delivers 133 boxes to 3 stores. Each store gets about the same number of boxes. Estimate the number of boxes going to each store.

   About ___44___ boxes

2. Quick Haul trucks can carry 9 boxes of one size. There is a shipment of 83 boxes to deliver. Estimate the number of truckloads for the shipment.

   About ___9___ truckloads

3. Quick Haul delivers 103 lamps to 7 stores. If each store gets about the same number of lamps, about how many lamps will each store get?

   About ___15___ lamps

Spectrum Division
Grade 4
Problem Solving: Dividing through 4 Digits by 1 Digit
75

75

NAME

💡 **Check What You Learned**

Problem Solving: Dividing through 4 Digits by 1 Digit

Read the problem carefully and solve. Show your work under each question.

Kenesha, Shawna, and Jake have postcard collections. They each plan to put their postcards into scrapbooks to organize them. Kenesha has 144 postcards, Shawna has 59 postcards, and Jake has 98 postcards.

1. Shawna only wants to use 9 pages of her scrapbook. How many postcards should she put on each page? How many will be left over?

   ___6___ postcards

   ___5___ postcards left over

2. Jake can fit 4 postcards on each page of his scrapbook. How many pages can he fill with his postcards? If he wants to put all of his postcards in the scrapbook, how many total pages will he need to use?

   ___24___ full pages

   ___25___ total pages needed

3. Kenesha plans to put 8 postcards on each page of her scrapbook. How many pages can she fill? How many postcards will be left over?

   ___18___ pages

   ___0___ postcards left over

4. Kenesha and Shawna decide to combine their postcard collections to make a collage. Each girl will get half of the total number of postcards. How many postcards will each girl get to use in the collage? How many will be left over?

   ___101___ postcards

   ___1___ postcard(s) left over

Spectrum Division
Grade 4
Problem Solving: Dividing through 4 Digits by 1 Digit
76

76

Spectrum Division
Grade 4

Answer Key

Answer Key

Page 77

Final Test Chapters 1–4

Divide.

	a	b	c	d	e
1.	9 ÷ 9)81	8 ÷ 7)56	6 ÷ 8)48	20 ÷ 8)160	6 ÷ 7)42
2.	3 ÷ 8)24	7 ÷ 5)35	4 ÷ 7)28	9 ÷ 6)54	8 ÷ 9)72
3.	110 ÷ 3)330	321 ÷ 2)642	103 ÷ 7)721	1621 ÷ 4)6484	108 ÷ 8)864
4.	90r4 ÷ 8)724	91r2 ÷ 7)639	200 ÷ 5)1000	41r1 ÷ 6)247	438 ÷ 2)876
5.	939r7 ÷ 9)8458	115r2 ÷ 7)807	114 ÷ 6)684	316r1 ÷ 3)949	678r1 ÷ 4)2713
6.	100r8 ÷ 9)908	255 ÷ 2)510	162 ÷ 4)648	986 ÷ 8)7888	300 ÷ 6)1800

Spectrum Division
Grade 4

Final Test
Chapters 1–4
77

Page 78

Final Test Chapters 1–4

Divide.

	a	b	c	d	e
7.	9 ÷ 9)81	6 ÷ 7)56	6 ÷ 8)48	20 ÷ 8)160	6 ÷ 7)42
8.	3 ÷ 8)24	7 ÷ 5)35	4 ÷ 7)28	9 ÷ 6)54	8 ÷ 9)72
9.	110 ÷ 3)330	321 ÷ 2)642	103 ÷ 7)721	1621 ÷ 4)6484	108 ÷ 8)864
10.	90r4 ÷ 8)724	91r2 ÷ 7)639	200 ÷ 5)1000	41r1 ÷ 6)247	438 ÷ 2)876

Fill in the missing numbers.

	a	b
11.	9 ÷ _9_ = 1	4 ÷ _2_ = 2
	90 ÷ _9_ = 10	40 ÷ _2_ = 20
	900 ÷ _9_ = 100	400 ÷ _2_ = 200
	9000 ÷ _9_ = 1000	4000 ÷ _2_ = 2000
12.	16 ÷ _4_ = 4	15 ÷ _3_ = 5
	160 ÷ _4_ = 40	1500 ÷ _3_ = 500
	1600 ÷ _4_ = 400	15000 ÷ _3_ = 5000
	16000 ÷ _4_ = 4000	150000 ÷ _3_ = 50000

Spectrum Division
Grade 4
78

Final Test
Chapters 1–4

Page 79

Final Test Chapters 1–4

Divide.

	a	b	c	d	e
13.	10r7 ÷ 8)87	10r3 ÷ 5)53	210r2 ÷ 4)842	60r6 ÷ 7)426	30r2 ÷ 3)92
14.	80r4 ÷ 6)484	104r7 ÷ 8)839	307r1 ÷ 2)615	10r8 ÷ 9)98	90r3 ÷ 6)543
15.	10r3 ÷ 7)73	120r3 ÷ 4)483	90r2 ÷ 3)272	103r2 ÷ 5)517	90r4 ÷ 7)634
16.	407r1 ÷ 2)815	60r4 ÷ 6)364	80r3 ÷ 4)323	90r6 ÷ 8)726	210r1 ÷ 3)631

Find the rule and complete each table.

17.

a

In	Out
32	8
28	7
8	2
36	9
40	10

divide by 4

b

In	Out
35	7
45	9
10	2
30	6
5	1

divide by 5

c

In	Out
56	7
16	2
40	5
64	8
72	9

divide by 8

Spectrum Division
Grade 4

Final Test
Chapters 1–4
79

Page 80

Final Test Chapters 1–4

Solve each problem. Show your work under each question.

18. A restaurant has 245 seats with 5 seats at each table. How many tables does the restaurant have?

The restaurant has _49_ tables.

19. Homer buys 3 newspapers every week. If Homer has 627 newspapers, how many weeks has he been buying them?

He has been buying newspapers for _209_ weeks.

20. A group of 30 children started a lawn mowing company at the beginning of the summer. At the end of the summer, the company had mowed 600 lawns. How many lawns did each child mow if each mowed an equal number?

Each child mowed _20_ lawns.

21. The Wilkinson family drove 1,374 miles in 9 days. How many miles did the Wilkinsons drive each day if they drove the same amount? How many more miles did they drive on the last day?

The Wilkinson family drove _152_ miles each day.

They drove _6_ extra miles on the last day.

Spectrum Division
Grade 4
80

Final Test
Chapters 1–4

Page 81

Final Test Chapters 1–4

Solve each problem. Show your work under each question.

22. Ms. Garrett had 40 guests at her birthday party. She cut her cake into 88 slices. Each guest ate 2 pieces of cake. How many slices were left?

There were _8_ slices left.

23. Lucy babysits for 2 families. She works the same number of hours each month for each family. If she worked 76 hours last month, how many hours did she work for each family?

She worked _38_ hours for each family.

24. Tom and Jose enjoy playing video games. Together, they play 10 hours a week. If they play 5 days a week for the same number of hours each day, how many hours do they both play together?

They play together _2_ hours a day.

25. At the basketball tournament, 28 people signed up to play. If there were 4 teams, how many players were on a team? Write a division equation. Then, solve.

_28 ÷ x = 4_

There were _7_ players on each team.

Spectrum Division
Grade 4

Final Test
Chapters 1–4
81

Page 82

Final Test Chapters 1–4

Solve each problem. Show your work under each question.

26. Howard Jackson scored 158 points this season playing basketball. He played in 7 games and scored about the same number of points in each game. About how many points did he score in each game?

He scored about _22_ points in each game.

27. Miss Gomez drove 256 miles in 4 hours. She drove the same number of miles each hour. How many miles did she drive in 1 hour?

She drove _64_ miles in 1 hour.

28. In the past 6 weeks, Jackson worked on 738 computers. Each week, he worked on the same number of computers. How many computers did he work on every week?

He worked on _123_ computers every week.

29. At baseball practice, 1,325 pitches were thrown to the players. If 5 players got the same number of pitches, how many pitches did each player get?

Each player got _265_ pitches.

Spectrum Division
Grade 4
82

Final Test
Chapters 1–4

Spectrum Division
Grade 4
96

Answer Key